OLDER CHILD ADOPTION

D1113368

OLDER CHILD ADOPTION

Grace Robinson

A Crossroad Book
The Crossroad Publishing Company
New York

1998

The Crossroad Publishing Company
370 Lexington Avenue, New York, New York 10017

Printed in the United States of America

Library of Congress Cataloging-in-Publication Data

Robinson, Grace.
    Older Child Adoption / Grace Robinson.
      p.   cm.
    Includes bibliographical references.
    ISBN 0-8245-1707-5 (pbk.)
    1. Older child adoption—United States—Case studies. 2. Adopted children—United States—Case studies. 3. Adoptive parents—United States—Case studies. I. Title.
    HV875.55.R63   1997
    362.73'4—dc21
                                               97-37545
                                                CIP

Contents

Acknowledgments

I am most thankful to the adoptive parents who shared their feelings, insights, experiences, and commitment with me when they were interviewed for this book. Their names, those of their children, and distinguishing characteristics have been changed to protect their privacy.

Many thanks also to the social workers who introduced me to these families and who provide them with caring and professional support.

I am profoundly grateful to Bernard and Joan McNamara, who read, commented, and made suggestions on the manuscript in an earlier form, and who guided me through the adoption experiences that led to my writing it in the first place.

Thanks too to Judy Downing, who began the project with me and encouraged me to carry on alone when I thought it was necessary to do so.

And of course I am grateful to Michael Leach of The Crossroad Publishing Company for recognizing the value of the book and getting it published.

Introduction

It is one thing to know about adopting an older child, and another to live with that child. In 1983 I was single and wanted a family. Within the next five years I adopted a twelve, a thirteen, and a nine year old. Soon after the first adoption I joined an adoption support group. There I met children who suffered from having lost their parents and siblings, who had been used for their parents' sexual pleasure, who had been beaten and lived in dread. I met parents struggling to secure educational, social, and mental health services for their children without becoming bankrupt. Sometimes I felt an urgency to give these children a voice, these parents a voice.

In the last several years I have interviewed the parents of thirty families in nine states and one province who adopted older children. The interviews indicated that my experience was not unique. This book is intended to give these parents a voice and, through their eyes, tell the story of their children. It also seeks to answer some of the questions brought up by living with children adopted when they are older. My reading tells me that some answers can be found in Lenore Terr's work concerning the effects of trauma on children; in recent studies about how children grieve after the loss of a parent through death or divorce; and in literature on attachment theory and the effects of sexual abuse, substance abuse, and adoption.

Older Child Adoption is the result of my experience and my research. It is for everyone who has considered such an adoption and wondered what it might be like to take the next step. It is also for those who have adopted an older child and wake up in the morning wondering what they have gotten themselves into.

In adoption literature the term *older child* refers to children who are older than two when they are adopted. Four of the children in this study were less than two when they were placed with their adoptive families in foster care or pre-adoptive placement. All were over two when they were formally adopted.

The families interviewed for this book adopted seventy-three children from the foster-care system and eleven directly from other countries. One sibling group of three adopted from the foster-care system had disrupted—*disrupting* means ending the parental relationship with the child emotionally and legally—from an international adoption. Had these eighty-four children not been abandoned, neglected, or abused, they would still be with their birth families.

According to the National Center on Child Abuse and Neglect, in 1994 there were 1,197,133 substantiated cases of the maltreatment of children in this country. Of these, 44.7 percent were neglected, 21.6 percent physically abused, 11.7 percent sexually abused, 4 percent emotionally maltreated, 2.1 percent medically neglected, and 15.9 percent abused in other ways; 26.7 percent were between the ages of two and five. Some received services in their family of origin to prevent removal; others entered the foster-care system. Of these foster children, some will eventually be returned to their birth family, some will become available for adoption, and others will remain in foster care until they reach adulthood.

Of the families interviewed for this book, seventeen live in the Eastern United States, three in the Midwest, nine in the West, and one in Canada. Names have been changed, but the vignettes used as illustrations throughout the book were extracted from the transcripts of these interviews. Though not direct quotations, the vignettes reflect the parents' own words and give entry to their minds, hearts, and homes.

Part 1 concentrates on the adopted children. In most cases they act out unresolved feelings about what has happened to them. At times they are sad, angry, scared, confused, enraged. Some feel rejected, inadequate, dirty, defenseless, hopeless, unlovable, alone. To work through such difficult feelings, children must feel safe. They cannot feel safe when they perceive that their living situation is temporary or that it depends on their behaving "normally." The long-term commitment of adoptive parents affords children the safety where their feelings can be expressed and worked through. Some acting out points directly to trauma, grief, loyalty conflicts, attachment disorder, or past abuse. Some is less focused, more difficult to understand. Whatever the behavior, adoptive parents must manage it but not take it personally. This challenge is described in the first six chapters.

Part 2 deals with how adoption, particularly older child adoption, takes the definition of nuclear and extended family beyond blood or resemblance, stretches the capacity of a community to provide services, and defines love as a commitment that transcends feeling and expectation.

A glossary of terms is available at the end of the book.

Throughout, *Older Child Adoption* seeks to make sense of some of the seemingly irrational behavior of the older adopted child. It gives the reader access to the living rooms and hearts of adoptive parents and children. It raises questions about present policies governing the services provided to such children and their families. Eighty-four children in thirty families in nine states and one province is too small a sample for statistical significance, but it not too small to provide insight into ways to improve the lot of children who, through no fault of their own, cannot remain in their birth home and of parents who adopt them.

Part I

Living with
the Older Adopted Child

I

The Traumatized Child

Most children adopted when they are older have been traumatized by their removal from their birth home. Such a removal is often the result of a traumatic event or ongoing abuse. Both affect the child, but the emotional aftermath of a catastrophic event is quite different from that caused by ongoing abuse. A catastrophic event wounds, but children who suffer ongoing abuse develop defense mechanisms that build a protective wall between themselves and others. While this minimizes further hurt, it also prevents the healing of wounds already inflicted.

Teresa was held in scalding water by her birth mother. Jody witnessed the murder of his foster father. These were catastrophic events. The more unexpected and catastrophic the event, the more vulnerable the victim is, regardless of age. However, the degree of trauma a person suffers depends not solely on the event but also on the victim's ability to defend himself or herself. The younger the children, the more vulnerable they are because their defenses are not fully formed. Adjustment to adoption requires the healing of the damage done by past traumatic events. Some children suffer from Post Traumatic Stress Syndrome, which is familiar to many of us as Vietnam Vets' Syndrome. All require the healing of their wounds and memories.

By the time most older children are removed from abusive families, their traumatic abuse has been ongoing. In these cases children have learned to expect abuse and to defend themselves against it by distancing themselves from their feelings and from other people. The problem is that their defenses are not selective—they defend themselves from the good as well as the bad. These defenses, which have served the children so well in the abusive situation, make them difficult to get close to. Have you ever tried to hug a porcupine? For children who have been traumatized by ongoing abuse, the healing of wounds and memories requires taming the porcupine.

The Healing of Wounds and Memories

The first step in the healing of a wound is becoming aware of it. Physical wounds are easy to see. Emotional wounds are not as obvious. After raising their birth children, the Newmans, who had birth children who had grown into adulthood, adopted several traumatized children from the foster-care system in the United States and from Overseas. Some of their adopted children's wounds were obvious from the start; others became evident as they lived together.

🐚 Teresa's whole bottom was burned. Her birth mother had held her in scalding water, then left her on a bed. Her grandmother found her three hours later. Her skin was already scaled. She must have been in shock. According to the medical report she almost died. Whenever anything happens she cries and cries, falls down, and just mourns. I comfort her.

Shirley Newman, about Teresa, three when placed, five now.

Not only scars but also perpetual mourning are the aftermath of Teresa's trauma. As the child mourns for her past hurt with every present one, she receives comfort for it as well.

Teresa's brother Paul did not have physical scars, but the Newmans learned from his bizarre behavior on his second birthday that he had also been traumatized.

🐚 When Paul looked up and saw a man he didn't know coming through the kitchen door, he screamed so loud I came running. I arrived downstairs in time to see Paul running around the corner, holding his foot, and throwing up. We don't know who did what to him, but the next time this friend visited Paul threw up again.

Monday I gave Paul and Teresa some chocolate cake and apple juice for a snack. Paul smeared it all over himself, the floor, and the cabinets. He had been here fifteen months. I sat him on a stool. It took three of us forty-five minutes to clean up the mess. I explained to him, "You can't do this. Look at all the work it makes to clean it all up." I knew it wasn't his fault, that something had come up.

Shirley Newman, about Paul, twenty months when placed, four now.

The arrival of this friend of the Newman's triggered traumatic anxiety in Paul resulting in an autonomic reaction, vomiting. It is possible that the smearing of the chocolate cake was a reenactment of earlier abuse. One of the degrading forms of abuse that some children have suffered is being smeared with feces. Perhaps Paul was one of these. Children act out pre-verbal abuse because they don't have the language to make sense of it. Later they may not have a clear memory of the abuse, or any recollection at all, but their body and soul remember. If unresolved, early pain and loss are still carried within a child, often erupting in unexpected ways that don't seem fully related to the current situation.

Drawings are sometimes a parent's entry into a child's traumatic past. Such was the case with Derek.

The second week Derek was here he had a temper tantrum like I'd never seen before. He screamed for hours. Phlegm came out of his throat, his face turned red, and he couldn't see us. I thought I had caused it, that I had done something awful to him, so when it was over we all went to McDonalds. After that it happened about two or three times a month, so I realized I hadn't caused it; it was something he had brought with him, the trauma of war and abandonment. He's drawn pictures of soldiers killing his mother and father, with blood all over the page. Repeatedly he draws a man putting him in a big box and another man coming to take him out.

Now a psychologist comes to the house—Derek's special friend. The more often he talks about it, the more often he has these spells. One of the theories suggests holding the child, but the psychologist said that if Derek has been sexually abused, touching him would make him worse. I now send him to his room and, if it gets really bad, the rest of us go outside.

Recently Derek took someone else's coloring book and marked all the pages. When I found out, I sent him to his room, but we had to carry him there because he started screaming down here. After he had been quiet for about ten minutes, I washed his face and said, "You color in someone else's book and get mad because I fuss at you? You can't do this." When he came out of his room he was embarrassed and looked around to see if anyone was going to make a comment. They did. "What did you do that for? You made so much noise." After a while it was all forgotten. It's scary, but he never hurts anyone else.

A while ago, when he was in a good mood, I said, "You know, Derek, when you do the kicking and screaming you make everyone mad at you. You are going to have to learn to control it. You are going to have to learn how to talk about it when something's bothering you." When I see him getting an angry look on his face I say, "Derek, think." He'll sit there for a while, looking like he's going off into space. Then, when he's back, I praise him and ask what he was thinking about. Sometimes he can tell me, but it's a while since he's had a tantrum.

Shirley Newman, about Derek, six when placed, eight now.

Scars, monotonous play, and a flashback told the tale of Richard's trauma. A flashback is the intrusion of the past into the present in ways that seem real. Flashbacks can be part of the residue of trauma.

❧ Richard was three and a half years old. When he came from Korea in January, I met him in the airport in Chicago. He had scars all over his body. We had six hours to wait for our next flight. Even though every time I looked at him he looked away, I felt that he was staring at me the whole time. During the first months at home he spent hours tying the legs of the chair together with string, then tying the chair to the table. I bought a skein and he spent hours unraveling it, tying things together, then untying them. He needed to do it for some reason.

That summer we rented a cabin by the ocean for vacation. When we arrived Richard went to look at the cabin while my husband and the older boys unloaded the suitcases. When Richard saw the suitcases he began screaming. I picked him up, carried him into the bedroom, and lay on the bed with him, rubbing his back to calm him down. He went into a trance and talked about his other mommy hurting him with knives. I assume that when he saw the suitcases he thought he was being sent back. That is the only time in my life I have wanted to kill somebody. It was a terrible feeling, but this was my child and she had hurt him.

When Richard reached school age, we took him to a psychologist because he had severe learning disabilities. The psychologist said, "He doesn't remember anything before the plane. For the time being he needs to forget. Forgetting takes a lot of energy."

Some time later when we were coming off a plane Richard said, "I remember a house with garbage on it." I didn't know what he meant until one day when we were looking at a picture of a thatched house. The thatching was what he called garbage. His terror when he saw the suitcases is the only memory I know he's had.

Shirley Newman, about Richard, three when placed, twenty-three now.

Richard's flashback showed his mother what had happened to him. It also made her aware that she is capable of murderous feelings, a difficult realization but one that enabled her to understand and to help Richard deal with his anger.

The school psychologist talked about the energy it takes to forget. All older adopted children have a lot to forget. For many this energy drain develops into behavior patterns similar to the organically based Attention Deficit Disorder (ADD). Children needing to forget and children with ADD have difficulty concentrating, poor frustration tolerance, are easily distracted, and have a limited attention span. They may use "spacing out," daydreaming, "hyper focusing," or compulsive activity to avoid the present or feelings from the past.

Some children who have been traumatized have stored angry feelings that erupt unpredictably not on the perpetrator of the trauma but on those close to them and on themselves. Matthew is one of these children. The Doggarts, who had birth children living at home and had adopted Josh, a special-needs child, adopted Matthew. Living with Matthew was scary.

Sometimes Matthew would run up, grab my neck, and give me a big kiss, but when I'd reach out to hug him back he'd claw me across the face. If we mentioned his mother's name he flew into a rage. A child might slap another, but Matthew would pick up a hammer and hit him over the head. He tried to kill the cat. I would grab whoever was hurt and send Matthew to his room where he would scream, jump on the bed, kick the wall. A lot of times he couldn't tell us why he was angry.

One day he took his life jacket off and jumped into the pool. The first time I didn't believe he intended to kill himself, but when it happened a second time we decided to get him into therapy.

Even though the state he had come from had agreed to pay for therapy when he needed it, it took a long time to get the funding in place.

It was a year after his adoption was finalized when he began talking about his past. He had flashbacks. One day when his brother was bumping his head on the trampoline Matthew said, "Ann used to drag me like that." Then he jumped for a while and didn't have to act out his anger because he had talked about it.

Last year, when Matthew was six, I was in the tub and smelled something burning. I wrapped the towel around me, went downstairs, and grabbed the stuff off the stove. "I'm going to burn this house down," Matthew said. The thing he hates most is to be spanked, so I said to him, "I am going to swat you three times, put you in bed, and you are going to stay there for a while." I felt shock and grief. What could have happened to this child to make him act this way?

After six months the therapist said he had done all he could do because Matthew wasn't remembering any more. He is seven and a half now and deals with his rage pretty well. He has a stump in the playroom that he will pound and pound rather than hurt someone.

Judy Doggart, about Matthew, four when placed, seven now.

The effort of the parent and child has to be twofold—behavioral containment for safety, and therapy for relief and healing. I say the effort of the parent *and* child because the child must work in therapy and allow himself or herself to be contained in order to be maintained at home. When a child shuts down in therapy and refuses to be contained, he or she becomes a danger to self and/or others. When this happens, temporary out-of-home placement is required.

Witnessing a murder is a traumatic event for anyone, particularly if it is the murder of a loved one. Jody witnessed the murder of his foster father. Jody was not the first older child the Kanes adopted nor the last. Jody's adoptive mother describes life with him this way.

I was really taken with Jody. I met him when I went on a field trip with my son Brent's class. Jody was an adorable kid with blond hair, blue eyes, and dimples. When he was eight he became available and we adopted him.

Jody was very difficult and time consuming from the first day. He did everything he could to get us to give him up and was shocked when we didn't toss him out. He was hyperactive, so I had him outside a lot where he could run and wasn't as likely to steal from me. Eventually it didn't set me off when he lied to me. I just said, "That's not true. I know you did it and so do you."

People have asked me, "How do you keep from laying hands on this child?" When I am mad I will not deal with him. I walk away saying, "I am angry at you. I can't even talk to you right now."

Through the years we have tried different things: time-out, positive reinforcement, negative reinforcement, behavior modification. I contend that if you have a child who desperately needs them, these techniques do not work. These are for children with a little bit of a problem. Jody's major acting out was urinating in the closet and on the carpet. We had him clean it up but that didn't keep him from doing it. He seemed driven to do it. If he was in trouble he'd go to his room, tear things up, and masturbate.

He became more aggressive in the wintertime because that's the season when he witnessed the murder. He stole his brother's toys and tore them up, we couldn't keep any money in the house, he cut a hole in our water bed. When I lay on the bed I heard the water, so I called for Jody, "You have to buy a kit with your own money and repair this bed." When he tore things up he had to pay for them or replace them with something of his. Eventually he didn't have anything.

Every now and then Jody would have a flashback. A few years ago when he was on the stairs I noticed his eyes looked strange. I said, "Jody, what's wrong?" He ran down the steps, grabbed the baby, brought her up the stairs, dropped her, and threw himself down in a huddle. It was a while before he could talk. A lot of times he'll become distracted, act out, or do something bizarre like knock a hole in the wall because he's fighting a memory.

Jody has been in therapy for years. Therapists work with him until they don't know any more to do, then they recommend someone else. Even with the subsidy, therapy is costly. Sometimes I'd have to drive him fifty miles to his appointment three times a week. It took a lot out of me, but I didn't think the other kids lost out because when Jody was doing well he was very good with them.

About every two years I'd get afraid for him and couldn't take any more, so he'd go to a residential treatment facility for a time. I had directories of facilities and made multitudes of calls. Never was I so desperate as to just put him anywhere. He would be gone for sixty or ninety days, after which he'd come home. We'd get pats on the back about the wonderful job we were doing with Jody and be told he was cured. He wasn't.

Eventually we found a therapist who had worked with a lot of Vietnam veterans. She thought Jody had Post Traumatic Stress Syndrome. When he was thirteen he had a flashback or a hallucination—it is difficult to know which one. He saw someone in the garage, and one day in the house. I heard crashing. Jody was throwing pool balls at the pictures. He started up the stairs hysterically yelling, "He's here. I'm not safe." When he finally calmed down he had no color. The therapist thought he had gone into shock. When Jody finally talked about it he said, "I know he's dead, but I'm telling you he was here." The therapist took him to the cemetery, back to the house where the murder occurred, helped him talk it out.

Some days we wondered if we could stand any more, but we were committed to Jody. I kept a diary, and if Jody did something really bad or really good I wrote it down. I made entries at least once a week. A lot of things that he did a normal child might do once or twice a day but he'd do fifty times. That's when it becomes wearing. Sometimes I would look back in the diary and see all the behaviors we don't have anymore and realize that he is changing. That would keep me going. And even though Jody tore things up, he never hurt anyone, and he is affectionate. I got enough positive back from him that I didn't take the things that he did personally. No matter where he was—on the run, in treatment, in a Department of Youth facility—I always got a card on Mother's Day. Even though he steals from me and lies to me, I know he loves me.

Karen Kane, about Jody, eight when placed, seventeen now.

Parenting a child who acts out his terrors is wearing and terrifying. Hallucinations are signs of psychosis. Visual flashbacks are signs of PTSS or dissociation. In either case the child and the family need help in dealing with the situation. If the placement is to survive, the parents need to feel they are not alone with the burden, and there have to be good times to balance the bad. In this situation there were some balancing factors. Jody was able and willing to give back. Jody's mom kept a diary from which she could get perspective and take comfort—this is bad but not as bad as it was a year or even a month ago. And Jody's mom felt part of a treatment system, able to find therapists and treatment centers when she and Jody needed them. She felt challenged, but she did not feel alone and without the resources necessary to parent Jody.

Flashbacks or hallucinations are not always accompanied by such acting out. Some children act in—they withdraw. They aren't battling ghosts, like Jody, but they are haunted nonetheless.

> Last summer when Sandy was sixteen I took her out West for six weeks. We took care of my sick brother. We were sitting in a hot tub one day when Sandy thought she saw the man who had abused her. It really upset her and she shut me out for several months. I think everybody should know that kids who have been traumatized can have confusion about what they see and whether it is real, and it doesn't mean they are crazy.
>
> *Ellen Valdez, single parent of one adopted child, Sandy, twelve when placed, seventeen now.*

Children who have been traumatized by a catastrophic event have experienced their own vulnerability. They can be immensely sad, like Teresa; terrified, like Paul, Robert, and Sandy; or enraged, like Matthew and Jody. For all of them, present-day events trigger feelings of traumatic rather than appropriate intensity. The result is that a parent's life can feel as out of control as the child's. It is impossible for parents of such children to be prepared for every eventuality, or to have the satisfaction of knowing that they "did the right thing." In such a situation it must be enough for parents to have done their best for the child, and then to take care of themselves and their marriage. Jody's mom put it this way:

> I have seen people adopt because they think it's a worthwhile thing to do. I think that everyone who adopts a child wants to do good, but you also need a deep desire to have a child. The only reason we could tolerate Jody's behavior through the years is that we were both committed to parenting him, so no matter what happened

we didn't blame each other and we were able to maintain contact in our marriage.

It was difficult for us to get away because it was hard to find a baby-sitter who could deal with Jody. He would put things over on them. When we got home there was always a problem, so we tended not to leave often. We'd put the kids to bed early and spend time together keeping things going in our marriage. There were days when I was too drained for anything so it wasn't like every day ended with a wonderful time with my husband, but you can get sucked into kids with problems until all you are is kids with problems.

We did go to Hawaii once for our anniversary. We were able to say, "Whatever happens will happen, worrying about it isn't going to change that." Jody stole a watch from a kid at school, and we dealt with it when we got home.

Before Jody I worried about things I could not change. With Jody I learned to put my best into every day but not to the point that I couldn't survive. I saved something for myself and my husband, and I prayed.

Karen Kane, about Jody, eight when placed, seventeen now.

Taming the Porcupine

The quills of the porcupine hurt those who come too close. So do the defenses of older adopted children who have learned from the trauma of abandonment and abuse that closeness hurts. They create distance by withdrawing and "numbing out," becoming superficially friendly, or being continuously oppositional. When parents reach across the distance either to take control of a situation or to be caring, older adopted children often respond in a hurtful or obnoxious manner. To feel safe they can't give up control.

Why is control so important? Either because they weren't cared for and survived by taking care of themselves, or because someone took away their autonomy in order to abuse them physically or sexually, or because they perceived their lives as out of control when the system moved them often and, in their view, capriciously. They want to stop the pain. They want to be in control.

The Hahns' adopted child, Fred, a three year old, had not been fed regularly, so he was used to taking care of himself when he was hungry. Being in control of food was one of his survival skills.

> At 6 A.M. the first morning Fred got up and helped himself to some ice cream from the freezer. The next morning it was half a bottle of children's vitamins. When we took him to the grocery store he wanted doughnuts, chips, and hot dogs. When we said, "We've got what we need, we're not going to get those things," he was all fists and feet kicking and screaming. We had never seen a scene like that in a public place. I wanted a T-shirt that said, "He's not with me."
>   *Aaron and Adelle Hahn, about Fred, three when placed, now five.*

Older adopted children not only don't necessarily look like their adoptive parents, they don't act like their parents' birth children would act. But then, they haven't had the experiences such birth children would have had. The early days of a placement can feel more like taming than parenting. As embarrassing as it is, this phase usually passes rather quickly.

What takes longer—and more courage—is dealing with the children's interpretation of the past as a way of discounting the present. Such cognitive distortions are aggravating defenses. Patience leaves them standing. Confrontation is more effective.

> The first of my four children who came when they were older, and brought their cultural background and baggage of memories, was my daughter Nan. She had been raised by her extended family in Vietnam until she was twelve, then came to this country with her mother. Her birth mother was not able to cope with living in a new culture, learning a new language, and having sole responsibility for her daughter. She started giving Nan to families for adoption, but Nan kept coming back home. A social worker asked me, "Will you take Nan? Her mother cannot communicate and has no idea what could happen to Nan." I agreed. In spite of everything, Nan came into the family with that wonderful Asian attitude: I will work hard and I will succeed.

We had some rough spots. For a long time I heard how beautiful Vietnam is and if it hadn't been for that stupid war, and if her father hadn't died, she wouldn't have to be here. Finally I exploded and said, "I'm sorry that there was a war, but I didn't cause it. I'm sorry your father died, but I didn't kill him. All that I am doing is trying to take a situation that wasn't good and make it good." Recognizing some of her ghosts in this way broke the ice and changed our relationship.

May Udall, single parent of several children adopted as infants and others adopted when they were older, about Nan, fourteen when placed, twenty-one now.

The traumas the children in the sample have endured are for the most part not natural disasters. They have been caused by people. In each case there is at least one perpetrator and one victim. Children will identify with one or the other on the way to becoming themselves. They will either take back the power by becoming the aggressor or play the victim role. Sometimes they get stuck in one or the other position. This played itself out with Barry and Jared.

❧ When Barry came he had bite marks and Jared had belt whip marks, so they had obviously both been victims of abuse. Barry was aggressive, assaultive, insulting, hyperactive, and extremely impulsive. Jared was distracted and withdrawn. By the time they had been here two weeks, Barry had thrown Jared down each of our three staircases—and Barry is half Jared's size.

Craig and Mitzi Clark, about Barry and Jared, three and four when placed, eleven and twelve now.

In the first two weeks of placement this is beginning play. The longer it continues the more embedded it becomes in the child's personality.

The struggle with most children is to move them out of the victim stance. They move out in small steps. Parenting them is a relentless war to end the tyranny of the past—the "I can't," or "I won't"—and to capture a new beginning,

❧ "I'm like this because of what happened to me," they say.
"Yes, that happened to you, but at some point you have to assume responsibility for your own life," I reply.

May Udall, single parent of both older adopted children and children adopted as babies.

❧ At camp one year a fifteen-year-old victim of incest was standing next to me. "My bathing suit won't to stay up," she said. There was nothing wrong with the suit. It fit well and was not stretched out. She was simply feeling like a sexual victim unable to stay clothed. Her twelve-year-old brother, on the other hand, kept disappearing with a ten-year-old boy whom he eventually molested.

Hope Walker, single parent of three older adopted children.

In this case two incest victims from the same biological family identified with opposite roles from the trauma. Being a parent trying to protect an adolescent choosing a victim stance is like trying to keep Jello in shape when the mold is removed before it's set. It's impossible. It is equally impossible to restrain the aggressor. Both of the adoptive parents of the two boys described in the last vignette felt something wasn't right and followed them whenever they were seen disappearing. The victim's dad was late coming upon them once; the molestation had occurred.

The most a parent can do is to provide enough structure for a safe environment and work with the child until he or she is capable of making the choice not to be a victim or an aggressor but a self. In several of the interviews parents have described it like this:

❧ People say to me, "Oh, my God, you must be so amazing to take these kids on." I don't take much credit for the two who are OK any more than I beat myself up about the one who's not. They make their choices. It doesn't have much to do with me as long as I'm doing my best. The rest is the tremendous amount of work that they have to do.

Elizabeth Packard; the Packards adopted a sibling group of three older children. The Packards were interviewed separately because they have divorced.

Sometimes the system is the aggressor and the families are the victims. At these times the children learn that the system, not the parent, is all powerful. When Andy became available for adoption some years after the trauma of his father's death, he was already a challenge. He became more difficult because of the way the system treated him.

Our pastors were working with a woman who had difficulty handling her seven-year-old son, Andy. His father had died of cancer when Andy was four, and Andy was a challenge. His mother decided to put him up for adoption. Our pastors called us to find out if we would be interested in adopting him. We had been married three years, had no kids, and the pastor knew that my wife had been adopted. We had talked about adopting, it was the desire of our hearts, but we thought it might be too soon. Andy's mom changed her mind and decided to keep him and get help. We were relieved.

Four or five months later the pastor called us from his vacation. Andy's mother had chased the pastor down. She'd lost control of herself with Andy and wanted to place him. " We can't find anyone else home. Can you keep Andy for a couple of days till we get back so he's safe?" At 10:30 at night we picked up this scared little boy who was hungry and hadn't had a bath in a week. The next day we got hold of the County Department of Social Services and told them that we had Andy and weren't licensed for foster care.

We asked, "What do we do?"

"Keep him. We'll get back to you." A week turned into a month. We called again.

"School is starting. What do we do with this kid?"

"Do whatever you need to do."

So we found him a small private school where there were eight in a class and he could get help. We started talking about adopting him and eventually called the County again.

"We'd be interested in adopting Andy. What do we do?"

County told us we needed a home study, so we found someone who does them and were told, "This is really backwards. We need to come and talk to you, but we need a referral from the County first."

So we were back to calling the County again. One month turned into two, and we were in a routine.

On the day his mother terminated her rights we got a call from the County, "We are going to come and get Andy because you are not licensed to do foster care."

"Where are you going to take him?"

"It's none of your concern. We are going to pick him up at school. What school does he go to?"

"I'm not going to tell you because you're not just going to come and take him out of school."

"We're going to send the sheriff out to arrest you."

"Do whatever you want, but you're not going to pull Andy out of class and whisk him away without an explanation. School is out at three. We want a couple of hours to tell him what's happening to him. Have someone here at 5:30." They agreed.

I called our congressman and he sent someone out, so the County DSS knew it was being watched. We had no legal rights, but we had had this child for two months and no one else was going to fight for him. We had been good enough for two months, why not for another week while the home study was done?

Eventually they took him, and he cried all the way down the driveway. Talk about tear your heart out! We were allowed to see him when it was convenient for the foster family, which was once. After two weeks and three weekends the home study was approved and he was back here. That move did a lot to damage the relationship between Andy and us. We had told him that he was coming back as soon as everything was straightened out, but we couldn't keep him from being taken away and now it's hard for him to feel safe with us.

Gail and Hector Garrett, the parents of three children adopted when they were older, about Andy, seven when placed, thirteen now.

There are other children in this sample who went to school in the morning, were picked up at dismissal time by their social workers, and were taken to a new foster home without warning, goodbyes, or their belongings. These experiences of how life is when someone else controls it, and how it feels to lose Mom, Dad, and siblings, make older adopted children more determined than ever to stay in control and isolated. Their defenses of not needing you; comparing the present with an imaginary preferred past; living the "I can't and you can't make me"; getting involved in secretive, hurtful behavior; and being endlessly oppositional are some of the quills that make it hurt to hug a traumatized adopted child.

2

The Grieving Child

Many people think that adopted children should not only be happy but even grateful. These people are looking at what the children have and are not considering what they have lost. For some parents, and all children, the way to adoption is paved with loss.

Among the parents interviewed for this book there are some who have birth children as well as adopted children, some who have not given birth but believe it's a possibility, some who have decided not to give birth because of genetic predisposition, some who are infertile, and some who have no partner. The last three groups make up more than half of those interviewed. At some time they have mourned the loss of being able to become parents in the usual way, of giving birth to their own flesh and blood, to the fantasy child who looks like them. These parents have passed through the stages of grief, accepted their situation, and decided on adoption as an alternative. One parent put it this way,

> Adoption is not our first choice. We're not just adopting kids because it's a nice thing to do. We have a need for kids, and for some reason life isn't the way we wanted it to be. It's not our first choice, and it's never theirs. They've had tremendous loss, and the loss will always be there. Just as any of us deals with loss, they have to go through all the stages and come to peace with it.
>
> *Elizabeth Packard; the Packards adopted a sibling group of three.*

What have children lost in the process of becoming available for adoption? All have lost birth parents; they miss the sense of belonging that comes from resembling the parents that are raising them, and the person they would have become had they remained with their birth parents. They no longer have the chance to have only one set of parents, like most people, and they cannot completely trust the parents they have because previous parents have been untrustworthy. Some have also lost siblings, foster parents, and the cultural, racial, and religious aspects of their heritage. In the case of some older children, abandonment, neglect, and even abuse have robbed them of the childhood they should have had. All of these losses need to be grieved.

The way children grieve will depend on their stage of development when they experience the loss, how frightened they were by it, their understanding of why it occurred, and whether or not they consider the loss reversible. Death is a final loss. Divorce is not. When parents separate, children hope they will get back together. Full grieving about the family no longer being together is delayed until this hope dies—usually when one parent remarries. When children are removed from their birth homes and placed in foster care, everyone hopes that it is not permanent. The plan is almost always to reunite the family. When the plan fails and parental rights are relinquished or terminated in court, children continue to hope to be reunited with their birth parents, but they aren't. They're adopted. Even so, that hope lives on because in most cases their parents are alive somewhere.

Because adoptive parents and children are at different stages of the grieving process, adoption occurs in an environment that is emotionally out of sync. When a parent dies and the family returns home after the funeral, everyone is sad together. The day children go to live with their adoptive family they suffer their most recent loss, that of their foster family. Adoptive parents, having had time to grieve their losses and having decided to adopt, are in joyous expectation of a new beginning. Their euphoria needs to make space and time for the child's grief. The child is moving in with strangers, a new family yet again, without having had anything to do with the decision. The following vignette illustrates this point:

❧ It was a crisp November day when I went to get Dolores and bring her home. My heart sang. Soon I'll be a mom. Dolores will be mine to protect, nurture, encourage, delight in forever. Half way to the agency the reality of what this day meant for Dolores came over me. Loss. Loss of her foster parents, birth brothers, foster siblings, home, school, and neighborhood of the past three years. I began to sob. I couldn't stop.

The social worker said, "Stop crying! What will Dolores think?"

"She'll think I know what's happening to her today," I responded.

Hope Walker, single parent of Dolores, twelve when placed, nineteen now.

Little children have few defense mechanisms so their immediate reaction to a new home is obvious to all. Children who are eight to ten months old have separation and stranger anxiety. That's their developmental stage. To lose a mother then, as Rudy did, feels life threatening.

✍ Rudy came when he was only eight months old, but we were his fourth family. When I'd drive, he'd reach for me and I'd have to hold his little hand. If I drove with both hands he'd scream, but if I touched him he was OK. When he was three or four years old I took him to the university preschool. At first I stayed two and a half hours, then I dropped back to an hour. Every time I'd leave, he'd scream.

Shirley Newman, about Rudy, eight months old when placed, five now.

As sometimes happens, Rudy took much longer than most children to move through the developmental stage he was in when he lost a parent.

Fear of the loss of a parent is very strong in the toddler, but its expression varies with the child. Paul was aggressive, and Brent withdrawn and fearful.

✍ We got Paul when he was twenty months old. The caseworker and foster mother brought him and stayed for three days. After they left, he screamed. For the first few days I changed his diapers as he stood there screaming. Half the time he would grab the diaper, step on it, and grind it into the floor. If we tried to touch him, he screamed more. What have I done? What's happened to him, I wondered. Two or three weeks later he let me hold him sometimes, but he'd still throw fits and scream at other times. His face was scary. Sometimes it got to me and I'd have to leave the room, walk around the house two or three times, or turn the TV on loud.

Shirley Newman, about Paul, 20 months old when placed, four now.

🍂 Brent came at twenty-two months; now he is seventeen. He was developmentally delayed, with some signs of fetal alcohol syndrome. I question whether he had been abused because he had marks on his arms and legs and was too good. For six months he instantly did what we asked. It was hard to get him to bed at night, and he had sleep problems. He had a few nightmares, but typically he just woke up and needed somebody with him. Sometimes when he seemed totally angry, he would get hold of my hair and I would have to pry his fingers open. That stopped after a year. Since then he's been a happy, regular kid.

Karen Kane, about Brent, placed at 22 months, seventeen now.

The older children are when they are adopted, the less obvious are their signs of grieving and the more entrenched is the pain. Some children, like Rafael, feel empty and overeat to fill the void.

🍂 Rafael weighed seventy-five pounds when he arrived and two hundred pounds two years later. He was stuffing his mouth with food and not doing any work on himself.

May Udall, single parent of Rafael, twelve when placed, seventeen now.

Sometimes so much energy goes into grieving that the children become disorganized. Such might have been the case with Lois.

🍂 Lois is a kid that never gets it right. If you ask her to get you a glass of water, you might get a glass of ice or pop. She really doesn't hear anything.

Carol Abbot, about Lois, four when placed, eleven now. The Abbots have an older birth child and five children they adopted after being their foster parents for some time.

Behavior such as this could also be a passive-aggressive expression of anger.

Older children quickly develop defense mechanisms. They numb out or block out the past.

🍂 Hillary came in October last year when she was seven. Hillary has no arms. She had been in an orphanage in a remote area of Russia.

She was brought to Moscow and her departure was delayed two weeks because of the paper work. She had the backpack and photo album we had sent her, and she wanted to be here. One day they told her they couldn't go because the plane was still broken. She said, "Then let's walk." But when she got here she acted as if she didn't want to be here. She walked into the house with big boots on, kicked everyone in the shins, and spit on everyone. I think that's how she defended herself in the orphanage. After three or four days of saying, "Nyet, nyet!" ("No, no!") I took her shoes off. Meanwhile I knew she was watching everything I did to see if I was an OK person because she was terrified. She settled in. In the summer two little girls, also from Russia, came over. Hillary didn't understand a word they said. In six or seven months she had blocked it out.

Shirley Newman, about Hillary, seven when placed, eight now.

As mentioned before, this blocking out takes energy and often affects school performance.

Children coming from a foster home where they felt loved often don't understand why they had to move and have strong reactions. To avoid getting sad they get mad and they believe what makes sense to them.

ꙮ   Heather was ten when she first came, and she was angry. She'd throw things, kick, and bite. I'd hold her—sit on her legs, hold her arms down, sometimes for an hour or more. She didn't misbehave if anyone was here, so I'd have company. At other times I'd lock myself in the bedroom to get relief, but she'd throw things at the door. When it got really bad I would cry and that overwhelmed her. She couldn't stand to see me cry.

We referred to her foster parents as Momma Grace and Daddy Tom.

"They couldn't adopt me. They were foster parents. Foster parents can't adopt."

Initially I didn't respond because I felt I had to protect her from the truth. Eventually I told her, "That's not true. They could have adopted you if they had wanted to. Your friend Melinda was adopted by her foster parents. Grace and Tom were the first people who ever loved you and treated you like a real person. They did care for you, and they still do, but they did not want to adopt you."

"Why not?"

"You'll have to ask them."

She got as far as telling them that she was angry at them.

A year later her foster parents adopted Annie, a foster child with whom Heather had lived in their family; they sent Heather an announcement. I knew that Annie had been with them since she was five days old, and that the adoption was going to be finalized. When the letter came from Grace and Tom, I was mowing the lawn. Heather brought it out to me. I started reading it, then realized what it said. "I don't have time to read this right now, I have to finish mowing before it gets dark." I told our therapist about it and he said, "Read it to her." Every week he'd ask me, "Did you read it to her?"

"No."

"Chicken?"

"Yes."

"Read it to her, because at this point she probably surmises what's in it"

So the night before we were going to see him again, I read it to her. There was no reaction. The therapy session went well. At the end the therapist commented, "See, there's nothing to worry about."

The following week Heather flipped out totally in school, crawling along the floor, refusing to do anything.

I remember Halloween that year.

"What are you going to be for Halloween?" asked the therapist.

"A baby."

"Why didn't I figure that out?" he laughed. And of course she had to buy a bottle and pacifier so she could practice before Halloween.

Babies are cute, babies are desirable, babies are safer. When she goes into crisis, she goes back to drinking her bottle. My friends think I'm crazy when she takes it out. "She has to start acting her age," they'll say. But I believe she has to live through what she didn't live through and get what she didn't get. We spent hours rocking when she first came because she said, "I need to rock." When she needs to be held, she'll say, "I need a hug."

One day after Heather had been with me a year, her former caseworker called while we were in a therapy session. Heather realized who it was and said she wanted to go back where she came from. The therapist said, "If you don't want to live here, you can go, but if you go, you can't come back. That's it. If I don't hear from you in twenty-four hours, I will call the worker and get you an airline ticket." I was absolutely horrified. While we were riding home in the car I said, "You realize that you won't go back to Grace and Tom. I don't know if you'll live in another foster family or be put in a group home."

"If I was in a group home they might hurt me."

"There might be people there who would hurt you, I don't know. I wouldn't be there to protect you."

"How would you feel if I left?"

"I don't want you to leave. I want you to be here with me."

Then she wanted me to find a phone booth so she could call the therapist and tell him she was staying.

Kerry Sadler, single parent of one older adopted child, Heather, ten when placed, fourteen now.

Sometimes children try to reverse the loss—to get sent back to their former caregivers. It can be important to give them a choice to affirm publicly the fact that even though they are still pining for the people and situations they came from, they are becoming attached to the people with whom they are.

❧ Kelly said she wanted to go back to her foster parents. We had a long talk, and I found out that she had gone up to the school. There were no swings. There were swings where she used to live. I put Kelly's clothes in a bag at the bottom of the stairs and said, "When you're ready to go, you tell me, and I'll take you back. But I want you to know that I love you, and I really want you here. Your foster parents couldn't keep you, so you'll go back to a different foster family, and maybe they'll adopt you. Who knows? But I really want you to stay here with me." I started crying. Maggie, her sister, started begging, "Kelly, please stay here. You're making a mistake." It took Kelly two weeks to decide to put her clothes back into her drawers.

Julia and Clyde Edwards, about Kelly and Maggie, a sibling group adopted together at seven and eight, respectively. They are now eleven and twelve.

One of the many facets of children's grief about not having one set of parents like everyone else is their pain that they were not born in the adoptive family. On this issue Richard is in the denial stage of grief.

🍎 Upstairs we have a lot of pictures framed on the wall. Richard would stand there and look at the pictures over and over.

"What are you looking for?" I'd ask.

"My baby picture."

"I didn't have you when you were a baby."

"Yes you did, I've always been your Richard."

Shirley Newman, about Richard, three when placed, twenty-three now.

Ann is openly sad about not having been a baby in her adoptive home, and her mother takes the opportunity to make this up to her.

🍎 One day when Ann and I were in the garage she saw the crib up in the rafters and asked, "Who slept in that crib?"

"Matt, Bob, and Cathy all slept in that crib," I replied.

"I'm the only one in the family who didn't sleep in it?"

"That's right."

For a couple of days after that Ann was really sad that she had not been a baby with us. When we were home alone sitting on the couch reading books, she brought it up again.

"Would you like to know what I would have done if you had been a baby with me?" I asked.

"Yes."

So I held her real close and pretended to be nursing her. She giggled, but she allowed it.

"And I'd burp you." I picked her up, this four year old with legs flopping all over, and burped her. I showed her all the things a mother does with a tiny baby. Several times she asked me to show her again, and I did. It was all she needed. The only time I see a little bit of sadness in her eyes is if something comes up and she'll say, "I don't remember that happening."

"You weren't living with us then," I'll reply, and she gets sad because she wants to have always lived with us.

I never mentioned doing this to anybody, not even the caseworker. They'd think I was crazy. Then I went to an attachment workshop. The speaker was an adoptee who was a therapist. He talked about parents of eight- and nine-year-old adoptees rocking them every night and giving them a bottle, so I guess what I did wasn't so nuts.

Katrina Adkins, about Ann, four when placed, eight now. The Adkins have two birth children and two children they adopted after being their foster parents for some time.

Sometimes you have to read the signs that a child is grieving, while at other times it's clear. In order to grieve openly, a child must feel safe enough to be vulnerable. This takes time.

❧ Regina came from Latin America when she was eleven. She had had polio when she was around five and had been in a rehabilitation institution ever since. There she received physical therapy, and knitted socks to make money. She had never been to school, never written or read Spanish. When she came she was very shy, had big iron braces on her legs, and had a hard time going to school. One day after she had been with us a couple of years, she broke down and cried, "Why didn't they come back for me when I got sick with polio? I was real little and they just took me to the doctor and left me there." I said, "Can you imagine what it would be like to be in an Indian village with a little girl who was so sick that she might die, and you take her to the big city hospital and the doctor says, 'If you take her back to the village, how will you take care of her? Leave her here'? I'm sure she loved you because you are a really nice person, but she probably thought the doctor knew best." That seemed to be exactly what she needed to hear.

When Regina finished high school I said, "Would you like to go visit your family in Latin America?"

"I can't go back. I have so much. I'm educated. They're poor. How could I just walk in and say, 'Hi! It's me! Bye'?"

She's thinking about it, but I don't know if she'll ever do it.

Shirley Newman, about Regina, eleven when placed, eighteen now.

❧ Pamela and Wanda came as foster kids and never went home. After six years they became available for adoption. They're precious children, easy kids—exceptions to the rule. There was no way we could give them up at that point, so we adopted them. We used to run into their birth mom at the store, but we haven't in quite a while. They always give her big hugs, and she calls Social Services every year and asks for pictures, but she stays out of their lives so they don't know her real well. Wanda and I were getting the pictures ready to send the other day, and I asked her, "Do you miss your birth mom?" Wanda teared up, so I let her cry, and told her, "I understand. It's OK." The past is there for all these kids, and it just doesn't work to deny it.

Carol Abbot, about Wanda, twenty-one months old when placed, nine now.

Parents must be open to the occasional overflowing of the well of sadness in their children, knowing that they can't take away the pain but only be with them when they feel it. The parents can't "fix it" or rewrite their children's lives. They must be prepared for the children to reexperience their loss at every new stage of development, because they have to feel through the new ways they understand it. In the middle years children wonder what was wrong with them that they were given up or abused. In adolescence they wonder who they are, given that they have two families.

Adoptive families need to go through the grief process until the child can accept having more than one set of parents and the parents can accept not being the only ones. This process of letting go and acceptance is described in the next chapter.

3

The Child with More Than One Mother

Becoming a parent arouses feelings of possessiveness—and therefore there is something very threatening about not being the only one. A baby is so dependent at birth that there is no challenge to the "mine," and most adoptive parents bond quickly. When adopting an older child, parents bring into their life a child who usually has lived with, remembers, loves, has been let down by, and is angry at other parents, particularly mothers. The most significant other mothers are the birth and psychological mothers. The adoptive parent can become a psychological parent, but some older adopted children have already had an aunt, grandmother, or foster mother who filled that role. It's not just that older adoptive children have another set of parents, it's that they already have a self. Although they might need you, they are wary. An adoptive parent describes the struggle.

- When a kid is born to you you've had nine months of preparation with a lot of loving going on, the whole thing happens organically, and you give birth to an infant who is going to love you. Adopted kids are complete strangers. There is no way they can have an emotional attachment to you right away. Our kids desperately wanted somebody to love them and they wanted to stay together as a family. My wife and I desperately wanted to have kids and wanted them to love us. But love has to grow by being expressed in the boring details of everyday life, cemented by facing crises and surviving together.

  I kept saying, "Come on now, let's get with the program." I wanted these kids to forget where they came from and who they were. Jose ran away a few times. The day David arrived he said,

"Yup, these are my parents," but it took him two years to act that way. Rosa took longer. It was hard because I was feeling they didn't like me. Some adopted kids do reject their parents: "Forget it. It isn't worth it. I don't love you. I can't do it." Most adoptive parents fall in love with their children, so when they reject us or part of us, it is at such a deep level that it really hurts. But more often we begin to realize that we are not being rejected; instead, we're being confronted with a life that already exists.

The reality of the old family in terms of the new one is tough for adoptive parents because we don't want to admit that the children's other parents had a positive emotional effect on them. Without that, they would be criminals already. Somebody—a parent, grandparent, aunt, foster parent—gave them enough love to get them to our door. They also gave them enough grief, which is an awful way to have children arrive. These kids have gone through pain that I hope never to have in my whole life and they still have some sort of hope, some sort of love. We need to nurture it, but we can't control it.

Instead of hoping that the kids will discard their old values and take ours, we help them identify and develop their positive strengths. They try to get us to buy their values, to say to their behavior, "This is really OK." Unfortunately, our kids from abusive backgrounds are into personal denigration, physical abuse, and confusing sex and violence. As a result, we had to go through a series of crises and change came in the aftermath. At any given time some of us are at logger heads, some in exile, some close to my heart, and that's how it is. That's my family.

Egan Packard, parent of Jose, Rosa, and David, thirteen, eleven, and ten when placed, twenty, eighteen, and seventeen now.

The struggle of the adoptive parent is not only to accept the fact that one can never replace the birth mother, but also to resist the temptation to want to be the only good mom, to avoid getting into an "I'm the good parent, the birth parent was the bad parent" mind set. The danger is that the adoptive parent will only criticize, never speak well of the other parent. Children assume that if their birth parents are bad, so are they. Consequently, the adoptive parent's way of talking about the birth parent affects the child's self-image. One mother handled it this way:

✍ When Millie and I talk about parents I tell her, "Parenting is not something that comes naturally. If someone gave me a pencil and told me to draw a cat, I wouldn't be able to draw anything that vaguely resembled a cat. I don't have that talent. But I can parent. We all have things that we can and cannot do. If people can't parent, it doesn't mean they are bad people, it just means they don't have that ability. Maybe your mom and dad weren't the parents you would have chosen, maybe your sisters and brother were not the siblings you would have chosen, but if you look close enough you will see something each of them has given you to make you the Millie you are today. You are not a bad person." Millie has an older brother who was brought up by his grandparents and two sisters who were in foster care. They don't want to see her. When her brother got married they didn't want her to go. That bothers me a lot.

Angela Jackson; the Jacksons have adult birth children and Millie, placed at ten, twelve now.

Sometimes contact with a child's birth family is disruptive, confusing, or creates torn loyalties. But contact with members of the birth family may also be able to give the child a sense of continuity and extended family. They can sometimes be an added resource for the adoptive parents, as Ben's grandmother is.

✍ Ben still has contact with his birth grandmother. She has become a grandma to all the kids. She buys them all birthday presents, makes gingerbread houses with them at Christmas time, comes to their soccer games. She's a real support person, and it helps Ben to have someone who's always been there for him.

Carol Abbot, about Ben, six when placed, ten now.

Former moms may live in the child's wishes, fantasies, and way of being. Contact with birth parents can make them real to the child, diminishing the tendency to fantasize. But some children and some birth parents handle the contact better than others.

✍ Donny and Lois not only see their brothers and sisters who have been adopted in other families, but they see their older brothers and sisters who were out of their birth home when Donny and

Lois were taken. And they see their birth mom a lot. The first time was an accident. We ran into her at a track meet at school, so I said, "This is your mom." For Lois it was great. "I know she's my mom, but you're my mom." It settled her down. But all of a sudden Don didn't know where he belonged. It's been tough for him. When he was invited to a birthday party where I thought he might run into her, we talked:

"How do you feel when you see your other mom?"

"I like to see her."

"Do you get sad when you have to leave her?"

"No."

Now he can see her, knows she's there, knows who she is, and so far when he gets angry and says, "I hate you, Mommy, you're the worst Mom in the whole world," he doesn't say, "I want to go to my other mom." We just have to deal with his anger because he's mad at me.

Carol Abbot, about Don and Lois, three and four when placed, ten and eleven now.

Some adoptive parents feel competitive with the birth parents: Will my child ever love me? Will I be his real mother? her real father? Parents feel they can love more than one child, but many don't consider that a child could love more than one set of parents. There is no replacing the birth mother, so competing for her place in the child's heart is useless and only adds fuel to the loyalty battle, putting obstacles in the way of attachment.

Sometimes birth parents give their children permission to love their adoptive parents. It doesn't take away the sadness for the child, but it does enable the child to become emotionally attached to the adoptive family without feeling disloyal. This is more likely to happen when the birth mother has chosen not to parent her child, as Ann's did, rather than when there has been a court termination of parental rights.

❧ Every once in a while Ann's birth mom calls. If Ann's home she'll talk to her; if not, I will. After the adoption we had a healthy goodbye visit with her birth mom and that helps. When Ann called her "Mom" she said, "I'm not your mom anymore. I'll always love you, but your new mom is going to raise you and take care of you." Ann really knows this is what her birth mother wants for her and that it's OK for her to love us. Ann also knows that I like her birth mother and when it comes up it's easy for me to talk about her.

On the other hand, it's hard for me to talk to Cathy about her birth mother because her parental rights were taken away from her. I know she didn't do what she needed to do to have Cathy, but I also know how much I love Cathy and if her birth mother has half those feelings it must be very difficult for her. She doesn't come up often, but when she does we talk about her.

Katrina Adkins, about Cathy, placed at ten months, eight now; and Ann, placed at four, eight now.

In some cases the reality, not just the feeling, of competition with past mothers is intense and pervasive.

❧ Nina, nineteen now, was fourteen when she came from El Salvador with her younger sister, Isobel, and brother, Rafael. When their mother died they went through three orphanages. When people die they become saints, and El Salvador became the land of milk and honey.

One day Nina remarked, "I didn't really have to come here. I just came to be sure Isobel had a home."

"You just came to be sure she didn't," I blurted. "You tell her that we're not family."

"I don't do that. I tell her you're not my family."

Nina fought everything. "I don't ride a bike, I'm too old." She went from refusing to get out of a skirt to wearing pants and two inches of make up. After discovering the Latino community she'd come home to our house full of black kids who were adopted as babies, and were here first, and say, "We Latinos are so much better." Everyone wanted to jump over the table and kill her. It got really hairy.

In school she told the teachers different stories, and one called up to say, "Nina would have done much better if she weren't so worried about her sister dying in El Salvador. With her father calling all the time, she wants to go back there."

"If she had a dad in El Salvador who wanted her, she wouldn't be here," I responded.

For her last two years of school Nina was in a work-initiation program. One day she was seen hanging around with the gangs in the metro. I called. Nina had not shown up at school, so I said, "If you think you're old enough not to do anything I tell you, this is it. You finish out the school year, find yourself a job, and get your own apartment." She went around telling everybody I was kicking her out, which I was. I heard about some people who wanted a nanny and were offering room and board and $100 a week. I told Nina, "I don't want you so far away that you'll never see your sister again, but Isobel doesn't know which of us is her mother, you or me. She's going into her teens and I don't want to have to fight you for the authority."

My relationship with Isobel has always been good. She's bright, affectionate, and was the first one to learn English. She wanted to belong, but Nina held her back. I hope now it will be possible for her to do what she has to do without feeling disloyal to her sister or her dead mother.

Nina started work reluctantly, but now she's blossoming! That and the fact that she's not in the house the whole time is changing our relationship. On Mother's Day she gave me a card.

"This is a really beautiful card, " I said.

"Did you read the words?"

"Yes I did. Did you mean them?"

"Yes. We've changed a lot in the last five years, and I realize that a lot of it is because of you."

Six months ago I would have written this sibling group off. They came from El Salvador, where there's not much hope. Education didn't open any doors for the people they knew, and many died young, so their attitude was, "What's the point?" It was a hard attitude to fight. Now I'm beginning to think all the results aren't in yet. Maybe this is a success story in the making.

May Udall, single parent of four children adopted as infants and four older, about Nina, Rafael, and Isobel, fourteen, twelve, and eight when placed, twenty-one, nineteen, and seventeen now.

Accepting a child's past and allowing past parents unlimited access are not the same thing. Children need consistency to feel safe and uninterrupted time in order to attach. They need to know who's in charge, and even when they're young they need to be allowed to make choices. The following segment of an interview with Fred's parents, given when Fred was five, shows how his parents, who adopted him at three, honored this process.

❧ One day Fred's birth mom was in town and called wanting to see him. "No, it won't work for me right now," I said. "We'll be happy to set up a visit during the Christmas holidays, and we would appreciate it if you would not contact Fred before that because he needs time to settle in." We asked Fred if he wanted to see her, and he said, "Yeah," so we set up a meeting on the Friday after Christmas. Fred's dad told him that I had asked his birth mother not to contact him until then. He started to cry, because he thought we were mean to say that.

"Fred, we did it because we want you to feel secure and know you have one mom and one dad like most kids. We don't want you to get confused. Confused children hurt their friends, hurt their teachers, and have a really hard time."

"Oh," he said, and continued to cry.

"Do you still think we're mean?" his Dad asked after a while.

"I don't think you're mean," Fred replied. "I think the words are really sad."

At 11:30 the Friday morning after Christmas we told Fred this was the day of his visit with his birth mom. We hung out and cuddled for a while, and then I said, "Fred, it's almost time. We need to get going."

"I don't want to go. Let's go later. Let's go tonight."

"We need to go now."

"Let's do it another time."

"If we don't go now we can't go until spring break because Mommy has to go to school. We might not be back here for six months."

"Let's come back in six months."

"Are you sure? You said you wanted to visit your birth mom and this is your chance."

"I want to play with Sandy."

"Are you sure?"

"I want to play with Sandy, then I want to go home."

"Then I'll go by myself and talk to her. Is that OK?"

"Yeah."

So we hugged and cuddled for a while. Fred was sitting on the sofa watching *Peter Pan* with the other kids when I left. He's been so much more settled since then. He really feels like our kid now. He's been so loving, really mushy with me, just smooching. It gives me goose bumps just thinking about it.

Aaron and Adele Hahn, about Fred, three when placed, five now.

This story doesn't end with, "And they all lived happily ever after." It just illustrates one step in the dance of claiming that adoptive parents and children do. An adoptive family is built step by step. Fred will see his birth mother again, and hopefully by then he will feel more secure in his adoptive family.

Older children who do not have contact with their birth families often fantasize about them and pine for them. Like Darcy, most don't want to leave one mother for the other; they want both.

🌿 Darcy has this dream that his mother is going to want him back, that she will come to live with us and take care of him again. "You'd let her come and live with us, Mom, wouldn't you?"

Ida Aldez, a single foster parent who adopted several of her foster children, including Darcy, two when placed, eight now.

Some adoptive children don't just dream about a reunion, they actively search. Some older children search because they feel lost and want to be found by their birth family before their adoption can be finalized. They fear that being adopted means that they will be lost to their birth family forever. Such was the struggle with Dolores, a twelve year old.

🌿 One day I found a telephone book left open to the surname of one of Dolores's aunts, so I knew she had begun looking for her birth family. Her mother had committed suicide, and this aunt had taken care of Dolores before and for a while after that. I didn't know where the family lived. We went to visit a friend of mine one evening and on the way home Dolores recognized her old neighborhood, "That's where I went to the dentist. That's where my brothers lived. That's where Grandma lives. Stop the car!" She got out and ran toward the building, which was a pre-war high rise. I got out and ran too, because I was afraid I was going to lose her in the building. I couldn't believe what was happening. Dolores had been with me only six months. We got in the elevator, went up, and knocked on the door of an apartment on the seventeenth floor. Her aunt opened the door. She hadn't seen Dolores in three years. We had the reunion, then Dolores got in the car to come home with me. No one had invited her to stay. She kept calling, "I don't want this adoption. Come get me." Nobody came. Finally in June she gave up and agreed to be adopted. We went to court and the adoption was finalized.

Hope Walker, single parent of Dolores, twelve when placed, nineteen now.

Some children don't give up until they are back with their birth family.

❧ Yetta was with us about six months when she was fourteen. She kept calling her biological family collect, and they accepted the charges. They wouldn't let her go, and she really wanted to go back to them. Finally her stepbrother came and tried to kidnap her. The situation was out of control, so for her safety we took Yetta to the airport the next day. My husband and I were very emotional, but I don't know if it was love. I think it was caring for her as parents, and some feelings of abandonment because she wouldn't let it work. We stayed with that emotion for about three months, then it was over. Yetta never turned to say goodbye. She was returned to the Children's Home and escaped from there to rejoin her birth family.

Dara and Chick Farley, about Yetta, fourteen when placed. Yetta was the Farley's third older child adoption.

For the Farley family, the fear of adoptive parents became a reality— Yetta would not or could not accept them, would not or could not adjust. Some children are not capable of attaching in the new situation. Yetta left, called the Farleys several times, but did not return. The break was complete. The Farleys could mourn and get on with their lives.

The situation most adoptive parents cannot even imagine, and therefore do not fear but sometimes have to survive, is living with the child who cannot detach or attach. Life becomes a series of glimmers of hope followed by devastation. In this case the adoptive parents are not just living with a child who has more than one mother; they are living with an attachment disordered or, at the extreme, an unattached child.

4

The Attachment Disordered Child

Except for those who have lost their parents through accidents or illness, or the very few whose parents voluntarily relinquished custody or parental rights, most children adopted when they are older have been removed from their birth parents because of neglect or abuse, and most have had multiple placements in foster care prior to adoption. From these experiences the children have learned that they can't trust adults to keep them, that there must be something wrong with them because so many people have given them away, and that closeness hurts because it is temporary. Consequently, they all have some difficulty becoming attached to others in a healthy way. To a greater or lesser degree, the basis of their attachments will not be affection but need. In some cases it will be the need to be taken care of; in others, it will be the need to take their rage out on someone. Such relationships are not reciprocal but destructive, manipulative, and at times, oppositional. The capacity for affection and empathy makes a person capable of concern for others, which is the basis for conscience development. This is why the development of the capacity for healthy attachment is so important and why it is imperative that children be raised in families.

Even the healthiest children moving out of the foster-care system will bring to an adoption the deep-seated need to know if this is "for real." They have lost so much so often that they are afraid to believe the new situation will last, so they protect themselves and test their parents.

🌢   Libby was afraid to get attached to anything, even her cat, because she was afraid she would lose it. The first time we took her and her twin sister, Leslie, to stay overnight at a friend's house (it was our wedding anniversary and we wanted some time alone), they thought we were taking them so these other people could look them over and see if they wanted them. We gave them two laundry baskets saying, "Pack the toys you want to take in these." Libby tried to get her whole room in the basket. She wasn't going to lose another life. They fought from the time we left the house until we picked them up to come home.

Libby and Leslie had heard about brothers and sisters in the foster-care system being separated, so they thought only one of them was going to be able to stay here. They set each other up, made up stories, told on each other, acted like they hated each other.

As they settled in, their testing behaviors increased in intensity and frequency.

"Maybe you'd be better off if I were dead," Libby said.

"No we wouldn't. We would cry a lot and really miss you. Leslie would get your dolls. We'd give your clothes to some poor kids, and I'd keep your pictures. Then I'd go back to work."

Libby decided not to kill herself. She talked about running away.

"If you think we're mean, wait till you see what's out in the street."

She woke up in the middle of the night still ticked off, but when she looked out the window it was dark, so she decided not to run.

The testing behaviors got so intense that the day before our weekly therapy session we told them, "Until you want us to be your parents, you can't call us Mommy and Daddy." That night we ate in a separate room from them. The next day we went to the Y as usual and told the woman who worked there what we were doing with the girls and why, so she would understand. Leslie, with her big brown eyes, is quite an actress. I'd send her to Hollywood, but she'd never write home.

"Oh, Mommy, can I have a hug?"

"No. You need to make up your mind if this is real or not. We'll talk about it when we go to the therapist tonight."

This upset the woman at the Y. She called Child Protective Services, so there was an investigation. When the child-protection worker talked to the children they said, "Mom won't sit at the same table with us, we are not allowed to call her Mom, she won't have us." The worker wondered why we had taken the children. She called the therapist, who said, "I haven't seen them this week so I don't know what's going on, but the children are emotionally disturbed."

This was the second time we had been reported, so we wanted the social worker to talk to everyone involved and make a decision in writing about our situation—either we take the children in and beat them, or we're good to them.

During the last three months it has felt like we've gotten through to Libby. I don't know how it happened. I guess we wore down her resistance like water on a rock. Now when I get upset with her, she cries real tears. She feels bad and doesn't know why. She used to say, "I love you" and hug from a distance, the "spaghetti hug." Now she clings.

Thelma and Mark Irwin, about Leslie and Libby, twins, four when placed, eight now.

Attaching in a healthy way to another person is a process of building trust. Sometimes adoptive parents feel that they always have to prove themselves and never have any trust in the bank. It's like a kid building a tower with blocks—he puts one block on top of another until he puts on one too many or puts it in the wrong place and the tower falls. Adoptive parents may feel for a time that their relationship with their child is secure, but then their handling of an event or the child's reaching a new stage of development causes a crisis. Then it feels as if the relationship they had established was an illusion and they have to start all over. This is illustrated in the story of Sandy.

Little by little twelve-year-old Sandy was able to bond. She let me feed her, clothe her, rub her back. Physical contact was very reassuring to her. So was food. One glass of juice wasn't enough; she drank the whole carton. She dressed like a truck driver—tough, in pants, preferably black. But she really liked getting new clothes, and because she was getting lots of things, she stayed. Her commitment was not to me but to making things work for herself.

There was a crisis once or twice a month. I wanted to talk everything through, so we had arguments. We screamed, yelled, and put several holes in the wall. A lot of emotion came out. I regret the holes in the wall, and I don't recommend arguments, but they did something for us. Now we have more of a relationship. We don't like to scream and yell at each other because it creates bad feelings.

After two years Sandy threatened to leave a couple of times. We were going to court to finalize the adoption, and she needed to make a commitment not just to being here but to beginning to care. She started saying things I hadn't heard since the first year, like "I miss my foster mom. I'm going back to her." I think her foster mom is a terrific lady, so it made perfect sense that Sandy would love her. I was jealous and hurt, but Sandy didn't go. We finalized, and then we only had a crisis once or twice a year.

Last summer I had to go away for three days to testify in a criminal case. Sandy felt as though I were deserting her. She did some destructive things—flunked some subjects in school, got mixed up with problem kids and let them steal my jewelry, left empty beer bottles and cigarettes around, had an ulcer flare-up and landed in the hospital. She said, "It was to get you. I did it because I didn't care." She wasn't at all friendly to me when I visited her in the hospital, so I'd go for half an hour each day and leave. The illness scared her, and everyone told her she had to get rid of the tension and not smoke or drink if she wanted to get better.

I gained more confidence in her because in spite of all her mistakes, she was still here. Now we take everything apart. Why did I do this? Why did you do that? What do we want? It's been five years in coming, but we can do it. No one is evil or bad; there are just unwise or destructive decisions. I don't think Sandy hides anything from me very long, and I don't hide anything from her. We trust each other now, but it took a long, long time.

Ellen Valdez, single parent of Sandy, twelve when placed, seventeen now.

Most older children resist closeness because they believe if they aren't close to anyone, they can't be abandoned. Being cared for by a parent throughout an illness can break through this resistance.

When Rosa first came she really didn't want to be here. She'd throw things at me and I'd catch them. "You don't want your hair dryer? OK, what else?" But Rosa had to have surgery. She came to us with a lump on her cheek the size of a pea. Within the first three or four weeks we decided to have it removed. The plastic surgeon took it off under local anesthetic. A week later I got a message that the surgeon wanted to see me, and being a medical professional myself, I knew the pathology report had come back. By the time I reached the doctor's office I imagined the poor kid hairless, dead, and buried. I figured this was it, cancer, and it was.

I remember going to her room to tell her the bad news. I told her about the bad cells and the good cells. Can you imagine living in someone's house for a month and having them come and tell you that you have cancer? She did pretty well with it. It looked ugly and kids asked her if she got hit. "No, I have cancer," she'd say. "Then they leave me alone," she explained to me. "I'll bet they do," I said.

The doctor hadn't gotten it all so she went into the hospital and had a huge patch taken out of her cheek and a graft taken from her leg. I had worked in hospitals for twenty years, but I had never spent the night there with my own child. It was horrible. She was miserably sick. When we took the dressings down, Rosa was looking at me. I think I could be more stoic than most, but it was not a pretty sight.

She had five procedures in a year to revise it. They put skin from behind her ear over it, kept excising it, checking the margins, and putting pieces in to make it look as good as they could. Now she has a little scar, a drag over the eye that makes her look sad.

Every once in a while she talks about it. If I look at the calendar it's always within a week of when it was first done. She has an amazing anniversary sense. She'll say, "Tell me again. What was it? If we'd let it alone would I have died? Is it really OK?" The experience of my seeing her through that, and really being there for her, helped us bond.

Elizabeth Packard, about Rosa, eleven when placed, now eighteen.

Some children believe that no one could love them and develop frustrating ways of shutting love out in order to maintain that belief. It protects them from becoming vulnerable but at the same time prevents them from getting the nurture that they need—and at some level want—but are afraid to allow themselves to receive. Losing love has given them so much pain that they'd rather not have love to lose.

❧ Ben decided that nobody really wanted him because everyone had given him up. His birth mother gave him up, his first foster family kept his sister and not him, the family who was going to adopt him decided not to after visits began. When he came here he was never with the group. If the kids were watching a show with us, Ben watched the same show alone downstairs. We had to work to draw him in. He'd sit back, wanting attention but never asking for it.

Our family therapist had suggested we tickle him as a nonthreatening way to force interaction. My husband would tickle the soup out of him.

"What do you want?"

"Attention"

"I don't believe you." So he got tickled some more.

"Attention!!!"

Eventually he started asking without being tickled.

Still he doesn't always accept the attention he gets. Ben is on a gymnastics team. He's really good at it but never smiles while he's doing it. My husband and I took him to a meet and spent the whole day with him. Instead of enjoying that he had all our attention, he was angry because the other kids got to stay home and play Nintendo. It's frustrating, but we'll keep on giving him attention, getting him to see that he's wanted.

Carol Abbot, about Ben, six when placed, ten now.

The lack of trust will show up in the annoying refusal to take the parent's word for anything—and in control battles. For the child, staying in control is a survival mechanism. It keeps at bay the powerless feeling of needing something and having to depend on someone who might not provide it, or wanting to stay somewhere and being moved without having any say in the matter.

🍃 Dennis depended only on himself. If I said, "Put your coat on," he would go outside to see if he really needed a coat. I wished he would sometimes do what I said without questioning it. When we took him to Germany he had to depend on us, but he remained oppositional. When we drove through Switzerland and Austria Dennis lay in the back seat playing with his doll. My husband wanted to show him the world.

"Dennis, I want you to sit up now and look out the window."

"You can make me look out but you can't make me see anything."

Darlene Olson, about Dennis, seven when placed, sixteen now.
In addition to Dennis, the Olsons have adult birth children.

To the degree that children are feeling angry, helpless, and hopeless all at once, they are full of rage. Many parents in the sample took physical control of their children when they began acting out the rage, because it was the only way the parents could think of to prevent their children from hurting themselves or others. Other parents held their children because they had read Martha Welch's book, *Holding Time*, or the work of Dr. Foster Cline, or because they had taken their child to a therapist who specializes in attachment issues who had taught them when and how to use this technique. Therapeutic holding is not the usual lap-sitting but a much more intense experience where the adult, either the parent or therapist, will securely but not punitively hold the child so that there can be eye contact, but the child cannot move without the adult's consent.

The theory behind this approach is that the rage state provoked by the closeness of the holding and the inability to control the situation takes the child back to the first year of life. Babies who are hungry, sick, or need changing cry out their distress, and if their mother regularly responds by relieving their discomfort and returning them to a relaxed state, the children begin to trust. For children whose mothers or primary caretakers did not respond regularly to their cries, trust is weak or nonexistent. The children become attachment disordered or, at the extreme, unattached. Holding a child until the rage dissipates into the relaxation of surrender to the parent can encourage the child to begin building trust in the parent.

Trust is crucial. But older children moving into adoption, especially those who have experienced neglect, losses, or trauma before their first birthday, have little basis for trust. In most cases adoptive parents of older children have no idea what that first year was like for their child. They only know that at some point the birth parents got so overwhelmed that they relinquished the child, or were so neglectful or abusive that the child was removed from them. In either case the journey to attachment in the adoptive family will be a struggle to re-parent the child through the rage-filled first year to the extent that it is necessary and possible. This involves the parents' taking control, the child's experiencing safety and caring, and the child's eventually being willing and able to yield control to the adoptive parents. This yielding indicates trust and the ability to allow the parents to parent the child. Without it, children will not accept the limits parents impose for their safety and

well-being. The ability of the child to accept limits is increasingly important as the child grows and becomes too big to be controlled.

Fred's parents adopted him when he was three, and he displayed
many of the symptoms of an unattached child.

❧ Everyone told us Fred was potty trained. He wasn't. In some ways
he was acting like a one year old, having tantrums like a two year
old, looking like he was four.

Fred couldn't handle time-out. He'd lay on his bed screaming,
"Mommy, Mommy, Mommy," but it wasn't for me, and I don't
think it was for his birth mom. It was for anybody, and it was
pathetic to listen to. He started throwing things around, so I put
him on a chair in the middle of the living room where I could see
him. He tried to break the chair. We had neighbors who had a two
year old and an infant. Fred hit them, hurt them, and snatched
their toys. He just pushed and pushed until I was on my knees,
"Stop! Stop somewhere!" We started spanking. It was something
we never wanted to do, but it was that or put him out in the snow.

One night I said, "I can't do this. I had a very nice life before
Fred. We were sad because we didn't have kids, but this is much,
much sadder for me." The maternal feelings in me were not being
fulfilled. Fred could never relax into being held, and when he did
hug me or try to kiss me, he kissed with his teeth and hugged in a
way that hurt. I felt I was being turned inside out and thrown
aside. My husband wasn't ready to give up. He thought that if we
exposed Fred to a good vision of life, good experiences, and were
honest with him, he would correct himself over time.

We decided to get help. In the Yellow Pages I came across the
Family Attachment Center, which specializes in the children of
adoption. We went to see the therapist, talked a few minutes, and
he said, "Let me show you what I do. Come here, Fred." Fred
went and sat on his lap. The therapist put his arms around Fred in
a restraining hold. Fred kicked and screamed like he was being
murdered. Then the therapist let go, and Fred just sat there. The
therapist said, "If this was a normal kid he would have been out of
my lap in a second and over sitting in yours. He's not attached.
That's the problem." He talked to us about rage reduction therapy,
showed us more about holding, and we went home.

"Forget it, we're not doing that," my husband said. "I don't want Fred totally dependent on external control."

"Maybe we should see the therapist and talk some more," I said, and went out. When I came home there was screaming in the bathroom. I opened the door, and my husband and Fred were sitting in the holding position.

"I thought we weren't going to do this."

"I didn't know what else to do."

The first few months it was very intense. Fred sweated and screamed his lungs out.

"You're breaking my legs!"

"Your legs are right here."

"You're breaking my pants. You're ripping my shirt." He lost his voice for days, and we hoped nobody called the police. The social worker told us to tell the neighbors what we were doing so they would understand.

"I am not going to let go of you, Fred, no matter what you do," was always his dad's response. A couple of times I let go. It was summer, we were in shorts, and Fred got really slippery and slid off me. I said, "Go to your room, I can't deal with this." It totally freaked him out, but I was afraid I was going to pound him.

The therapist pointed out that Fred's lack of attachment to anybody had promoted a pathologically early development of self will. By the age of three he was, in his own estimation, an emancipated being. He had not gone through the normal progression of depending on and surrendering to a mother and father. Neither his birth mother nor birth father had provided for him, so Fred had learned that if there was going to be anything for him, he had to get it for himself. Anything that stood in his way had to be obliterated. If we tried to impose our needs, our schedule, and he wasn't ready for it, it was an automatic fit. Last night Fred's dad was on the sofa with him for over an hour, and Fred was fighting 90 percent of the time. Fred and I had had a really cozy day. Then I went to use the computer, and he was with his dad. Fred started wailing for me like he was being tortured.

"Mommy, come out here and sit with me." I came out. Then he wouldn't focus on connecting with his dad, so I went back to what I was doing.

"Mommy, come out here!"

"Fred, when you get connected with Pa, I'll come and sit with you." Whoever is holding him is the bad parent. When I'm holding him he calls for his dad. When we're both holding him, he calls for the dog. Sometimes he threatens: "I'm going to call the cops and they'll come get you." Or, "I'm going to call Santa Claus and tell him not to bring you presents." Or, "I'm going to call my real mom and tell her you're not being nice to me."

Last night he said to his dad, "I'm going to run away to the grocery store, and when you follow me you'll cross the street and cars are going to roll over you again and again and again . . . and the people from the school will run over you again and again and again. . . . There are nails in the road and they are going to poke up through your eyes. They're going to get you in the ambulance and take you to the hospital and they won't be able to fix you."

"Yeah, I'll be dead. I'll just be dead."

"Yup, you'll be dead."

"Then the garbage men are going to come and take me to the dump and the birds are going to eat my remains."

"Yup, they're going to peck your eyes out."

"And then I'm going to get up and come home and we're going to sit on the sofa and have holding time until we get connected and we're happy again."

There was still more rage after that. It's scary, and I'm not sure whether we should go with it like we did last night or cover Fred's mouth, which we've done at other times. When Fred and his dad finally got connected his dad said, "You hurt my feelings by telling me how the cars were going to run over me and the birds were going to eat me, because when you say those things you really mean them. You can see them happening to me."

"Pa, I just say those things when I'm mad."

When Fred comes out of the rage he always hugs and is very loving. He has gone from physically hurting to using words to express his anger, and we see that as progress.

But there are still times when both of us reach bottom and lie in bed at three in the morning with eyes wide open saying, "This might be too tough for us." Then three hours later Fred pitter-patters in, jumps on the bed, cuddles, and sometimes gets on my stomach under the covers and pretends to be born to me over and over. Then we get up saying, "We're going to make it."

Thelma and Mark Hahn, about Fred, three when placed, five now.

The most important part of the holding is the closeness afterward. The parent has taken total control, holding the child close and safe throughout the period of rage until the child yields to the parent's control and relaxes. Then parent and child are loving and cuddly. The child experiences that even his terrible rage, which frightens him, does not scare his parent away, does not result in the parent's abandoning him. Trust begins to grow. Usually this process needs to be repeated many, many times. As difficult as this method of reaching a child is, for many it gives hope.

There are attachment disordered children who will not rage, or who will rage but not capitulate. Those are the unreachable ones. The heartbreaking fact is that they can accept the treatment for a time and then stop, as one mother found out.

❧ After Curt's first hospitalization he was placed in a day treatment school where we had rage reduction therapy once a week. It gave Curt an outlet for his anger, so he was able to live at home. When he'd get angry I'd say, "I know you're really angry, but we can't deal with that unless we have help." He'd hold it until 10:30 on Wednesday morning. He was ten years old, weighed sixty pounds, and it took four of us to hold onto him. When it was over we had some soft, close time when he would trace my face with his fingers, and we could look lovingly at each other like mother and child. The rest of the week he'd come home from school, beat the trees until supper time, then we'd eat and read or play a game together. On weekends we did planned activities like hikes or visits to a museum or friends.

After two years he began to act weird. He got his head shaved, and one day when he got home before me I caught him zipping his fly on the front lawn. The therapist and I knew he had a secret, but we couldn't get it out of him. He held out even through the rage-reduction therapy. He would rage but not capitulate. There was no soft and cuddly ending. He'd get up and flip the light switch as he went out, leaving us in total darkness. Symbolic and very sad.

Hope Walker, about Curt, nine when placed, twelve now.

Unhappily, there are children who are so damaged that they will not allow anyone or anything to reach them. Such was the case with Darcy.

🍎 Darcy had been in one other foster placement for a month and came to our house the day he was two. He would sit on my lap but never get close. All I know about his early life is that his mother would drop him off with someone, saying, "I'm going to the store," and not return for weeks. Now it was impossible for him to count on anybody.

Darcy was six before he was legally free for me to adopt him. During that time his social workers kept changing, so nobody got to know him. Most of them never even saw him, and those who did found it difficult to believe what I said about him. Darcy is a handsome boy, charming when he wants to be. But his preschool teacher said, "I'm seeing the things you're seeing, and I'm really worried." Darcy had a look in his eyes that told me there was something wrong.

I had him evaluated, and the evaluator said, "You spoil him. You need to put him in time-out." At first I'd have to hold him in the time-out chair and he'd hit, scream, kick, and bite. Now he'll go, but he'll say, "I can't wait till I'm big enough not to have to obey any rules anymore."

I read Dr. Foster Cline's list of symptoms of children with attachment disorders and Darcy has all but one. He doesn't talk about feelings, never sheds a tear, and has a lot of rage inside that never comes out in appropriate ways. He'll hug me, but only for seconds, and it feels artificial. He will hug strangers, especially men. He's been very cruel to animals and other children. He takes good care of his stuffed animals, but he's ruined most of his toys. He breaks other kids' toys, especially if it's one they really like. He wanders through the house at every hour of the day or night touching everything. He steals and lies about things that he's done even when I catch him. He acts as though he doesn't have a conscience. I found an attachment therapist who lives 230 miles from here,

and we did holding therapy. Nothing genuine came out of Darcy—
he usually went to sleep.

As Darcy got older he got more dangerous. He was fascinated
with fire, knives, and killing. "I can't wait till I'm big enough to
stab you," he said to me one day when he was seven, and almost as
tall as I am. Darcy's therapist told me that Darcy might not be able
to live at home, that he might need a residential program. I felt
guilty, that I must have done something wrong. I had had sixty or
seventy foster children throughout the years and I couldn't understand why I couldn't handle Darcy. Finally I called the Department
of Social Services and said, "If you don't do something to help me I
am going to have to disrupt the adoption and Darcy will have to go
back to foster care." I got respite care every other weekend.

But my two youngest were getting too old to be kept in the
playpen, to be kept with me, to be kept away from Darcy. He did
things like put thumbtacks on the rug where the baby crawls. I
started hearing myself yelling at the kids. I finally realized that no
matter what I did to make it work, Darcy sabotaged it. The Department of Social Services moved Darcy into a therapeutic foster
home, and he comes home two weekends a month. When the therapeutic foster parents say that Darcy has to leave, he can't come
back to my house if things aren't straightened out. He doesn't
need to come back here and do something to hurt somebody. The
social worker said, "You'll have to go to court and declare that it's
unsafe for your family, or that you're not fit to take care of Darcy."

"For the survival of my family I know I can do that."

"You know it would really damage him for you to put him back
in foster care. He'd be bounced from place to place and end up in
a residential center."

"That's where he belongs right now. The state is going to end
up paying to support him for the rest of his life if he doesn't get
the right help now."

"We can't worry about what's going to happen down the road.
Our budget is really tight this year."

There are places that do ninety-day evaluations and prescribe
the kind of treatment the child needs. Then they say, "Take him
home, because such a placement is not available."

None of these places even admits that attachment disorder is a
diagnosis. If he doesn't get help Darcy will be in an institution

until he's eighteen and eventually end up in prison. Even though I know in my heart that I have done everything I can for Darcy, I will be sad if I have to disrupt the adoption to keep my family safe and make it possible for him to have what he needs.

Ida Aldez, a single parent, about Darcy, two when placed, eight now.

This vignette gives in a nutshell the situation of a family with an unattached child. Darcy was placed at two years of age with only one other placement between the birth family and the fost-adopt situation. Even a limited number of disruptions for a very young child can be traumatic. Early diagnosis and appropriate treatment for attachment disorder such as Fred is receiving might have made the difference between a child being able to grow into a responsible member of a family, and a child who will be a dangerous burden to society.

A child without a conscience usually grows into an adult who can commit criminal acts without remorse. Accurate diagnosis and sufficient money available for treatment early in a child's life means fewer jail cells needed for the adult he or she becomes. It also means early detection of children whose ability to trust has been irremediably destroyed, those for whom living in a family is not an appropriate plan. Being able to triage in this way will make older child adoption safer for adoptive families.

As one parent put it,

§ There are some kids who have a poor prognosis. If you take one of them you need to know that he'll burn your barn, kill your horses, and probably not feel bad about it. But there are other kids that deserve a chance. The problem is finding out who's who.

Earl Raleigh, single parent of Casey, thirteen when placed, eighteen now.

There is another factor that makes it particularly difficult to develop a diagnosis and determine attachment problems. Children suffering from brain damage caused by substance abuse during pregnancy, particularly when it is combined with poor nutrition, sometimes have some of the same behaviors as children with an attachment disorder. They make repeated mistakes, misbehave in a way that seems deliberate, tell "crazy" lies, have language problems, and lag behind in conscience development. But these behaviors are caused by prenatal neurological damage, not early environmental damage, although some children have suffered both. The bonded child with prenatal substance-abuse effects acts impulsively but cares very much about the consequences of what he or she has done. This caring gives parents something with which to work.

These children may benefit from a very structured approach at home and school that includes supervision, reminders, cues, and coping techniques. They can learn to compensate for their problem areas to avoid repeated failure and trouble. But above all they need direction, encouragement, and support to find, develop, and enjoy their strengths and interests. These will bolster their self-esteem in the face of so many challenges, relieve stress and perhaps develop skills, talents, and hobbies for leisure and employment in the future.

The effectiveness of this approach will depend on the extent of the brain damage suffered in utero. In the case of moderate to severe brain damage the symptoms will only respond to treatment to a certain point. It is important for parents to know what can and cannot be done, to know what success looks like on a daily basis with a given child, and to rejoice in it even if no one else recognizes it.

For children who are not organically damaged by parental substance abuse but whose ability to trust has been diminished by their treatment during their first year of life, a structured approach can be helpful in terms of child management, but this is not enough to heal attachment problems. Specific and often intense work to rebuild trust or build it for the first time is mandatory, because it is the foundation for reciprocal healthy relationships that lead to developing the capacity to care and to internalizing values.

5

The Sexually Abused Child

No matter how young or old a person is, a victim experiences sexual abuse as a violation that penetrates to the core. Adult victims are overpowered and find their defenses inadequate. Child victims are betrayed by trusted grown-ups. The result for all victims is a profound feeling of vulnerability in a dangerous world.

The severity of sexual abuse depends on several factors. The higher the level of aggression and the more invasive the abuse, the more severe it is. The younger the victim, the less able the child is to defend himself or herself. If the abuser is in a position of trust, more damage will be done to the child's ability to trust other adults, including the adoptive parents. If the abuse has gone on for a prolonged period of time, the child will have developed defenses against being emotionally touched by the abuser or anyone else. If the child is young enough, and incest is the family's way of nurturing each other, love and sex may become synonymous for the child. Love, sex, and violence or aggression may also be confused. Adoptive parents may never know exactly what happened to their child, but they live with the effects.

🐦 Be ready to recognize the earmarks of sexual abuse and neglect because this is the cradle and nursery of our kids. When your kids present you with a really slimy way of relating, it's an affront to you personally, although that may or may not be the way they intend it. It's hard to adopt a detached enough stance to just deal with it, but you have to. "You can't do that here." "I won't accept that you treat women that way, or men that way, or yourself that way."
Egan Packard, parent of a sibling group of three.

Children who have lived in incestuous homes, where the nurturing touch was sexual, continue to seek nurturing in sexual ways. It's all they know. They need to learn other ways of getting their nonsexual needs met.

✖ We got Sandra when she was two and a half years old. We were her tenth home. At first I saw her as a very clinging, needy child who had never been filled up. There were signs that something sexual had happened to her before the age of two—public masturbation, inappropriate vocabulary and touching of other people, sexual acting out with her siblings. In her play therapy she acted out some situations that the therapist said confirmed our beliefs. She wasn't able to treat the child, but at least we knew what we were dealing with. For a while when Sandra started to masturbate in the den or kitchen area, I'd send her to her room. "Those are private acts. You do them in the privacy of your room." If I'd walk by her room and find her masturbating on her bed, I'd just pull the bedroom door closed. She was spending more and more time in her room doing these things. Eventually I realized that what was going on wasn't healthy, so when I would see her masturbating I would say, "I see you are needing some extra attention. You need to be close to Momma. Come in here and help Momma in the kitchen." Or maybe, "Do you need extra touching? Let's go rock and I'll rub your head." She is able to be appropriate with me most of the time, but sometimes I have to say, "You're not going to sit here and touch me that way. If you want to stay with me, you have to do it this way." Sandra's seven and a half now and still needs a lot of physical contact. She crawls into my lap and lays my hand on her head for me to stroke her hair. At church sometimes she'll lay across my lap and say, "Rub my back, Mommy."

Chad and Amy Bowers, about Sandra, two when placed, seven now. The Bowers have five older adopted children.

Children understand the world through the filter of their experience, and if their relationships with parents have been sexual, they will carry that into the adoptive family.

✖ When we got girls who had been abused I had to watch everything I said and how I dressed. I had to wear pajamas, close my door, and lock it going to the bathroom.

When I came home from work Kelly would jump on me, hug me. Maggie wouldn't let any part of her body touch me except for her hands. A kiss was a peck. I'm a hug man, so I'd say, "I get a hug and a kiss from Mom, a hug and a kiss from Kelly, a hug and a kiss from the dog, and I get nothing from you."

"Oh, Dad, I'm sorry, I was busy."

We'd go shopping and I'd try showing them so much love and attention. I'd walk with one of the girls, and my wife would walk with the other one. I'd hold Maggie's arm crossing the street. She'd continue to hold my arm, then my hand, and the next thing I knew she was insinuating to my wife that we were on a date. I was trying to have fun and talk to them, but they were getting the wrong impression, so that had to stop.

Kelly masturbated in front of my brother. Once when everyone was watching TV, she walked from one end of the room to the other, playing with herself the whole distance. That's what they did in the birth home where they were sexually abused by their mother, father, uncles, and aunts.

One day a week we went swimming, then to therapy, then home to eat. Kelly wouldn't put her underwear on, then she'd talk to the therapist with her legs wide open. The therapist commented, "Oh, we have no private parts today. What do we feel about these private parts? There's nothing there, so there's nothing to hide?"

Every week after swimming I would say, "Kelly, you've got your underwear on, right?" because I didn't want to be embarrassed again, and every week she'd do it, yet still deny the sexual abuse.

Clyde Edwards, about Kelly, eight when placed, twelve now, and Maggie, seven when placed, eleven now.

Kelly and Maggie had been bound to secrecy and Kelly was beginning to let the secret out with her actions. She was testing the waters—I want to trust my adoptive parents with this information, but can I? Maggie was still bound by the secret. Julia Edwards tells more of the story.

❧ One day a twelve-year-old girl came to our house and started talking about how her mother's boyfriend sexually abused her. So I said, "I'm very proud of you, that you can talk about this. If you can talk about it with the social worker at school, you'll be able to work it out, and when you become seventeen or eighteen you'll have a good life. My kids who were eight and nine were listening, so I said, "But there are children who can't talk about things like this, and they're going to have a really hard time when they grow up." Then we got in the car to go to therapy.

"Ma, I've got to tell you something," Kelly said.

"What?" I asked.

"Shut up!" Maggie shouted.

"Maggie, I don't care if you don't want help, but I want help. I want to make sure I'm OK when I grow up. My uncle . . . "

"Shut up! If you tell, you're telling on me too." Maggie punched Kelly right in the face. I intervened,

"Kelly, you're really going to have help if you tell this to the therapist. I can be your mom, and I can comfort you, but I don't know what we should do about this."

About four sessions later it started to come out. The more Kelly told, the worse it got for Maggie. She said Kelly was lying, that her biological parents were good. She pushed Kelly down the stairs. Then she pushed my five-year-old nephew down the stairs. I couldn't understand what was happening to Maggie. I started disciplining her more. She had to look words up in the dictionary and write their meanings. She was afraid to go out, so whenever we were supposed to go somewhere, she would do something so she couldn't go. She cut up her dad's favorite sweatshirt, cut the sleeve right off, and not at the seam. Then she tried to convince me that I did it. "I'll buy you five hundred sweatshirts, Dad, but I didn't do it. I just want to get out of trouble."

One day Maggie was angry with me. She was downstairs, and I didn't hear anything, so I sent Kelly down to see what Maggie was doing. She was sitting on a pile of laundry playing with a lighter. This kid was deathly afraid of fire, but Kelly was telling too much, so Maggie decided to set a fire and forget about everything. I called the therapist, "What should I do? I don't know what to do right now." He said, "Take her to the hospital." So that's what I did. I sat there for five hours, and they wouldn't take her. I said, "I'm not moving from here. Either you take her or call Child Protective Services. Do something, because I'm not taking her home with me. What if I hadn't felt something was wrong and sent Kelly down to check on her? What's going to happen if I'm not there? I cannot trust her in my house." So they finally took her.

Julia Edwards, about Maggie, seven when placed, eleven now.

The secrecy that surrounds sexual abuse heightens the tension of guilt involved. The pressure of Kelly's talking had been too much for Maggie. Hospitalizing Maggie was tough on both parents. Two hours later they were both in the waiting room, crying.

☙ "I'm her dad, we're getting her out and that's it." The hospital staff said, "We'll let you know when she can leave." I felt shattered. I hated their parents for what they had done to these kids, and I was angry at my wife because I thought she should be able to handle it. "I've got my business. You want kids, you're supposed to be the mom who can handle this." It was more than I could stand. . . .

Our family therapist didn't think we should take Maggie home because she was still denying what had happened to her. He suggested another hospital, one that has a unit specializing in children Maggie's age. We got Maggie transferred there and eventually she started talking. "Do you see these bruises on the bottoms of my feet? That's where he beat me with the bottom of a brush." They put her on Haldol, a pretty strong medication, and she began imagining things. "My dad came after me completely naked, chasing me with a knife." The dad had my face, so I almost got into trouble. Our family therapist explained to everyone that in the dream it was my face because I'm the safe dad. That was her mind's way of making the dream less scary.

Clyde Edwards, about Maggie, seven when placed, eleven now.

Maggie wasn't the only child in the families interviewed who had such a dream with the adoptive father's face superimposed on the aggressor. This is the unconscious protecting the child, but it can compromise the adoptive parent as much as fabricated accusations. This is an area of legal risk for the adoptive parent. Some children fearfully misinterpret nonsexual situations as sexual. Some have flashbacks or even hallucinations and confuse the past with the present. Some children in their pain and rage deliberately accuse others falsely of abuse.

Adoptive parents also risk catching bad feelings. Victimized children have a way of smearing their feelings on their adoptive parents. Sonya's mother describes it this way:

❧ Sonya's a snoop. She can tell me where everything of mine is. It gives me the creeps to know she's been through all my things. And I get slimed by her. If she's going to touch me, I push her hand away. I don't trust her. The other day we were up in my room. It was time for the dogs to go out. Sonya sashayed out of my room like a slut, like a Las Vegas show girl. It made my body crawl. I felt she was aiming it at me, so I said, "Maybe your biological mother wanted you sexually, but I do not." She said she was unaware of it, but I don't believe her. It's an uncomfortable feeling.
Dara Farley, about Sonya, twelve when placed, seventeen now.

This provocative way of acting can lead to a child's being victimized again. In the case of child molestation, whether it's incest or not, the taboo has been broken by an adult, by someone older and bigger, or by someone smarter or more socially adept, leaving the child feeling defenseless. The safeguards of society did not prevail. If children abused in this way do not work through these helpless feelings, they will be endangered by them. They will not be able to set limits within which they can feel good and safe. If all parents need to teach children how to defend themselves, how much more must this be done by the parents of those who have been victimized. Muriel's mom worked hard at this.

❧ We adopted Mitchell and his sister, Muriel, when he was twelve and she was seventeen. Muriel is retarded. Shortly after they came, they went to a decision making group run by the Department of Human Services. Muriel met a young man at one of these meetings, and when they got home Mitchell said, "Mother, you need to talk to Muriel. She met this guy, and she was kissing him. She wasn't just kissing him, they were lip-locked. You need to do something about it." I talked to Muriel and called the supervisor, who agreed not to let them be alone together. I spent from June until the opening of school talking to Muriel about not letting anybody talk her into doing anything she didn't want to do, what was safe, and what rape meant. After school started we were driving into town and she said, "I need to tell you something."

"What?"

"When I was in the other foster family, Bing raped me."

I can remember thanking God that it was dark so she couldn't see my expression. I didn't think she knew what she was talking about, so I asked her to describe what happened.

"One time when everybody was home, I went to use the bathroom. I started to lock the door, but Bing said, 'Oh, you don't have to do that,' so I didn't. As I pulled down my pants to go to the bathroom, he came in and pulled my pants down more and got on top of me on the floor. You know what, Mom? Bing has a bone in his penis. I was screaming. Mother came up the stairs yelling. Bing got off me and ran into the bedroom, and Mom came in and blamed it on me. I tried to tell her what happened, but she didn't believe me."

"Why didn't you tell your caseworker?" I asked.

"I was too frightened."

I was very angry about this and called DHS. They called the police.

I kept telling Muriel, "Nobody has the right to rape you. It's against the law."

"How come the police aren't doing anything?" she asked.

I called the investigator and he said, "You may press charges, and it will go to court, and it will be his word against hers. They don't feel there's a case, so they're not going to do anything."

I was really upset. It was hard for me to talk to my husband about it because he said, "What good will it do?" She was out of danger, and that was the issue for them, and I could understand that. But I needed to prove to her that people don't have the right to treat her that way, and that there are consequences. I'm not sure she ever got that, and I wondered if they would have treated her this way if she wasn't retarded.

This kid has been a victim her whole life, and it's really hard to turn that around. I fear for her. If we watch a movie about rape on TV, I use it to give her concrete examples about how she can protect herself, and they work on it a lot at school.

There have been a few incidents at school. I used to drop the kids off early, and they'd sit in the gym. The boy she had initially kissed goes to the same high school. He started talking to her about sex and showing her some pictures. She finally got scared and went to talk to some of the teachers. He got suspended, and they couldn't be together.

Another time she had a summer job as a janitor's helper. After she was finished, she had to walk to a friend's house where I would pick her up on my way home from work. One day three boys who had teased her at school were driving down the road. They stopped and said, "Muriel, want to have a ride with us?"

"What did you do?" I asked.

"I didn't pay any attention, and I kept walking to my friend's house."

"That's wonderful" I said. I really feel that she's picked up on a lot of things.

Ginger Lancaster, about Muriel, seventeen when placed, twenty now.

Muriel was taught how to avoid potentially harmful situations and keep herself safe. This is quite different from being able to stay in an abusive situation without feeling the hurt. The first is a life skill. The second is a defense mechanism that is useful during the abuse but then must be discarded in order to reach out so there can be positive relationships after abuse.

What happened to Leslie and Libby denigrated them. A great deal had to be done to raise their self-esteem, and their parents had to live with their defense mechanisms until the children didn't feel the need for them anymore.

❧ When we met Libby and Leslie they were living with their teacher temporarily. Libby had gone to school with black-and-blue marks all over her where her foster father had beaten her with a wooden spoon. When asked what she had done the day before, Leslie had described the sexual games her foster mother and grandmother had played with her. Even though Leslie and Libby were only four, this was the second time they had gone to school and not returned to the same home.

Libby and Leslie were twins who had been molested by their grandmother, mother, and the mother's boyfriend. Their older sister peed on them, their mom pooped on them and wiped it over their faces—all kinds of degrading stuff that made me sick. It was no wonder that when they came Leslie would sit and say, "I'm just a dumb, dumb retard." She ate with her hands and wet herself without even knowing she was doing it when she was under stress. Once, after my son had left after a visit, we went shopping because I thought they would feel bad and this would help them. They sat down to wait for me to pay for the merchandise and Libby said, "Leslie, you're peeing all over everything." I looked and there was a stream and she was not aware of doing it.

Dissociating from that part of her body was one of Leslie's defense mechanisms. She also shut down if she thought there was no recourse. That's why she was classified as retarded. I tell her, "We know you're not dumb, so you're not going to get away with that here."

Now we have a new set of problems. She's starting to be willful, to fabricate stories, and she's just as capable of getting into trouble as Libby. When I ask her, "Why did you do it?" and she says, "I don't know," I respond, "I don't accept that," but I don't push the point. I don't want her to shut down. The door hasn't been open that long.

Leslie has made tremendous progress from fifth to sixth grade, so we have had "emotionally disturbed" dropped from her classification. Now she has resource room for only two subjects, language and reading.

Thelma and Mark Irwin, about Leslie and Libby, four when placed, eight now.

Dissociation is an adaptive defense mechanism we all use to block out our surroundings in order to attend to the business at hand. Children involved in ongoing abuse can learn to dissociate to an abnormal degree in order to escape overwhelming emotions like feeling abandoned and intense physical sensations like being beaten or sexually overstimulated. Such children, like Leslie, learn to go someplace inside themselves where they can avoid feelings—both physical and emotional. In this case the departure of the Irwins' grown-up biological son stirred up feelings, perhaps of abandonment, which resulted in Leslie's dissociating from present reality—including the feeling in the bladder and urethra that informs us when we need to or are urinating. As children feel safe in their adoptive families, they have less need of these defense mechanisms and learn more appropriate ones. Occasionally, however, a present event will activate intense past feelings and sometimes the defense mechanism used to cope with them will reappear.

Before adopting an older child, most parents are able to read whatever records are available so they know what has been written about the child's history. A formal psychological evaluation with a projective test can be useful in providing insight into a child's feelings. In living with the child, parents learn much more both through symptoms like flashbacks (intense visual memories intruding into the present) and through body language. Most adoptive parents cannot imagine what could have happened to cause their children to be the way they find them. These windows opening onto the past can nurture parents' empathy, giving them energy to endure the present.

✺ One night we sent Libby up to bed around 7 o'clock, and when we went up about 9:30 we found her standing on the landing, shaking. I put my arms around her, picked her up, and she started crying. An hour later she was still crying. A song on the radio had touched her off before she went to sleep, and what her birth mother had done replayed in her head. Her birth mother had lent the carpenter her bed and three-year-old daughter to thank him for fixing a door.

To this day Leslie gets nervous when we take her picture. If we take more than one picture, her face changes. She gets a guarded smile, a smirk, and we can see the tension in her. It means she is about to crumble, and if we probe, she will. I am sure that cameras have been used with her in some way during abuse.

Thelma and Mark Irwin, parents of Libby and Leslie, four when placed, eight now.

Ignorance of the past and assumptions we make about the present can make it difficult for adoptive parents to shield their children from pain. The past lies in wait like land mines in a field after a war. Children also return to issues again and again as they reach new developmental stages with new skills and understanding. This makes a child's process of healing from trauma and loss more like a spiral than a straight line.

It is not unusual for abused children to feel that they did something to cause the abuse, particularly if it occurred during the preschool years.

This results in their feeling anxious and guilty. Incidents can trigger the return of these feelings as flashbacks.

❧ I had signed for the school to do an occupational therapy test on Heather. During that test they made her undress to see if she could button and unbutton. When I picked her up from the baby sitter that afternoon, Heather said, "I unbuttoned my clothes, but I didn't take my underwear off. Did I do the right thing? Was it OK that I did that?" We went through two weeks of her having severe nightmares every night. Because I was so angry, I waited for a week before I wrote the school. I told the principal that I was holding her responsible because she knew Heather's background and should have informed the person brought in to do the test. Had she said, "I'm really sorry this happened. I'll look into it and see that it doesn't happen again," I would have dropped it. She didn't, so at the end of the CSE review I brought it up.

"I'd like it on record that the parent signed for the evaluation," the assistant principal responded.

"I signed to have my child evaluated, not traumatized. Do you know what it's like to spend two weeks watching your child lie on her bed whimpering and rocking back and forth, terrified that she has done something wrong? You people are responsible for that."

"You're getting angry."

"You're right. I'm angry. You should have checked into this. This is not the only sexually abused child in this school system. A sweater could be brought that the child could put on. There are dolls that lace and tie and button. This should never be done to another child."

After this I told Heather, "No one tests you without my being there."

Kerry Sadler, single parent of Heather, ten when placed, fourteen now.

Parenting a hurt child is a constant effort to protect that child from further hurt. It is necessary to set very clear guidelines with schools and professionals in other areas concerning what a child can tolerate and what is intrusive. Written advice from the child's therapist can help avoid the denial or lack of sensitivity some adults display.

Parenting hurt children also means caring for them as they experience the feelings brought up by the anniversaries of past events, past hurts.

🌑 The beginning of the year is very bad for Linda because it brings the time when the perpetrator gets out of prison that much closer. That's difficult for her to handle. She is uncomfortable with any strange man. I have to accompany her and talk for her with the dentist and doctor. When a teacher approached her too fast, she put her hands up, "Don't hit me!" It's odd, because when she's alone, she thinks she's in control of everything, and on the street she'll talk to anybody. She wants everybody to know how big and strong she is. "If you were as hurt as I was sexually, you would be very careful about what you did. You wouldn't want to get hurt again."

> *Phyllis Tate, single parent of Linda, eleven when placed, fourteen now.*

Sometimes an anniversary reaction will be kicked off not by the calendar but the season.

🌑 Every Halloween the three boys went haywire. At first we thought it was all the scary things about the holiday. Then we wondered if it could be an unconscious response to the anniversary of their traumatic abuse and removal from their home. But that was in December, so we thought, no, that's not it. Then we realized that the boys were living in the Southwest when this happened, where fall sets in much later than here in the Northeast. The boys were reminded of the trauma by seasonal cues rather than calendar dates.

> *Natalie and Brady O'Mara, about Tomas, Fabio, and Jose, placed at ten, eight, and six, now twenty-two, twenty, and eighteen. The O'Maras have two birth children and eleven children adopted when they were older. Four of these were international adoptions.*

Living with a sexually abused child is not easy, and introducing one to a family with other children is a serious step to take. Parents need to be able to make an informed choice. This requires that they are told all that is known of a child's history. When facts are withheld it is a disservice to everyone concerned.

A six year old named Lena came to live with us in pre-adoptive placement. We had told the social worker that we could not deal with a child who was emotionally disturbed. We could handle one who needed behavior modification but no more. When Lena had been with us three weeks, she relived her sexual abuse in very graphic terms. We couldn't put her in therapy without the permission of the state because we hadn't adopted her yet. Once they knew that we knew she had been abused in the system, they didn't return our calls. We called the school. Lena had told them about the abuse the previous spring. She had told them at the camp she attended that summer, and she was kept in the same home until we took her in November. She had been just visiting with us, and one weekend I refused to take her back to the foster home because she was so terrified of returning there.

Soon after that she started going after my boys and telling my girls all they ever wanted to know about sex. I had to be on my toes all the time. I think she did as well as she could in the situation, but I realized I had bitten off more than I could chew. Returning her to the Department of Social Service was the hardest thing I have ever done, but I knew I couldn't go on with it. She was a very sad, hurt, damaged little girl.

Georgia Collins, about Lena, age six. The Collins family has several children adopted when they were older.

In a situation like this, social workers have the difficult job of discerning what is true and what is confused or exaggerated. Appropriate homes are scarce. When they see a parent doing a good job with difficult kids, they look upon that parent as a resource. Perhaps the social worker placing Lena felt that even though Georgia Collins didn't feel capable of parenting such a child, she would find she could do it given the opportunity . . . or that once the child was placed she would feel too guilty to disrupt the adoption regardless of how difficult the situation became, so the placement would hold.

The fact of the matter is that even when the parent is told everything the social worker knows, this is just the tip of the iceberg in terms of the reality of the child's past life and its effect on the present. The more prepared the parent is for the child, the less likely the adoption is to disrupt. Parents need to be given realistic information and if possible have personal contact with families who have adopted children with similar backgrounds to the child they are considering. One of the conclusions of a study done at Rutgers University is that the closer the parent's picture of the child is to the child they actually get, even when that child has significant problems, the less likely the adoption is to disrupt. Knowingly hiding information from the prospective parent can saddle a capable and generous parent with an undeserved sense of guilt and failure, and return to the system a child even more difficult to place because of another move, another rejection.

In a case like Lena's, there is also the possibility that the other children in the family will be hurt. At best, children who have been sexually abused need more external structure to be safe, given that sexual taboos have been broken. At worst, they may have already become perpetrators. For all concerned, honesty is the only fair policy in this situation.

Sometimes parents discover by accident that more structure is necessary. The life of parents of children adopted when they were older is full of surprises.

❧ I walked in the bedroom one day. Clayton and Lucille were in bed facing each other, and Kerry was on top of them. Since then we don't leave them alone together, ever. The two younger ones go to an after-school sports or study program until we pick them up at six. It takes planning and money, but we can't trust them alone here together.

Edsel and Marcia Dean, about Kerry, Lucille, and Clayton, placed separately when they were five, eight, and four, now eighteen, fourteen, and twelve.

❧ When Celeste first came she ran around without clothes. Very quickly we told her, "No one is interested in your body." One time we were in Chicago visiting my husband's parents. Celeste was completely naked, sitting on the bed. She was flaunting it, and her brother was outside the room, very interested.

"Celeste, what are you doing?" I said. "You don't have modesty? Basic decency?"

"You have a dirty mind," she replied.

Joy and Bud Zack, about Celeste, ten when placed, sixteen now. Celeste is the oldest of an adopted sibling group of four.

One of our girls was sexually assaulted by her older brother here in our house. He assaulted not only his sister but our other two girls and one of the boys. His anger took over, and he struck out at the kids. Lois told me about what had happened a couple of days after he moved to another adoptive home.

"I don't like him, " she said.

"Why not?" I asked.

"He tried feeling down my pants."

He had done it to four out of the six. I called his mother, and she called social services. They started to deal with it in therapy, and the kids needed to deal with it in therapy before he and his new family moved away. We had them all together, and he started off in a corner. They had to say they were angry at him, and he had to say he was sorry. When it was over they were all friends again, but he had lost trust with the kids. There is no way I would leave them alone with him again, but at least we know, and he knows.

Carol Abbot. The Abbots have five adopted and one birth child.

Sexually abused children can grow into healthy selves, but they can also remain victims or even become perpetrators of abuse. Those who become perpetrators take back the power they were robbed of during the abuse by identifying with and becoming the abuser. Not all perpetrators of sexual abuse were sexually abused themselves, but some have been. According to C. T. Johnson, a specialist in the field, the exposure to and experience of violence may be an even more significant influence in developing abusive patterns of behavior.

When David was fourteen, the baby sitter couldn't handle him. He was running all over town after school. We asked an adult neighbor if she would like him to help her with her small children. We didn't know that he had been sexually abused. When he reached puberty, he repeated what he had suffered. The four year old told his mother, so hopefully it was the only incident. When the mother called, we did not know what to do. We called his therapist at midnight, and he said to bring David in the next day. At first David said, "You can call the police, I don't care, I didn't do it." Eventually he admitted it to the therapist.

Later that summer David ran away for three days. He was seen at the summer camp with two young children.

"What are you doing?" a camp counselor asked him.

"Baby sitting," David answered.

The people at the camp knew what David had done before, so they called me at work.

"He's not baby sitting anybody," I said.

I called his therapist and said, "We have to do something before someone else gets hurt."

Reluctantly, he agreed, and I called the crisis center.

The psychiatrist who evaluated him said, "David is detached from reality. When I talk to him, he looks far away and takes a long time to answer. I cannot in good conscience send him home."

Our neighbor pressed charges for the sake of getting David help.

While David was in the hospital we had family counseling. First it was the two of us with David, then Celeste, his sister, with him. David denied having been abused. Celeste said, "I saw it. I saw it with my own eyes." He admitted it after that. Now Celeste goes to a survival group for teenagers who have been sexually abused. She admitted she had been abused, and they didn't put her down because they all have suffered.

After David had been in the hospital two months they wanted to discharge him. I said, "He cannot come home. I have three other kids at home. I work outside the home, so I cannot be there all the time. What if he hurts his sisters?"

The probation officer told me, "If you do not want to accept him home, they cannot force you."

After four months in the hospital, David was sent by the court to a residential school for long-term treatment for those who have been sexually abused and are now abusers.

Joy and Bud Zack, about David, twelve when placed, eighteen now. David was adopted with his three siblings.

Two things of great importance in this vignette are the neighbor pressing charges and the parent refusing to have the child return home after four months in the hospital. A brief hospital stay may provide a diagnosis and temporary respite to stabilize the child so that he does not pose an immediate danger, but it does not fix deep-seated problems. It can be the catalyst for change, but it does not itself make the long-term changes that are needed in cases like those described here.

Often people who are friends feel uncomfortable pressing charges. They may feel that it's not something a friend would do. Sometimes the parents of the victim don't want to press charges so the victim will not have to testify. It is essential that charges be pressed both for the victim and the perpetrator. The victim needs to know that what was done to him wasn't right and that the law will protect him. The perpetrator not only needs to know that society will not allow such behavior but that he needs help. Most treatment programs for sexual perpetrators require that the juvenile entering the program has been adjudicated. The treatment is very difficult. The specter of prison as the alternative to treatment must be very real to enable the perpetrator to persevere through the pain of taking responsibility for his actions and allowing himself to feel empathy for his victims.

Psychiatric hospitals are places for diagnosis and crisis care. Because of the current financial climate, managed care and other health programs are requiring that in-patient care, if approved at all for reimbursement, be very limited in time. When the crisis is past, the hospital wants to discharge the patient. Often the hospital recommendation will be, "The child needs residential care but none is available. Take the child home until a bed in an appropriate treatment facility becomes available."

𝕾 After Maureen had been in the hospital several weeks the staff said to us, "She is out of control and violent. We can't handle her. You'll have to take her home until you can find residential placement."

I said, "Wait a minute. You have trained professionals coming in eight-hour shifts around the clock, restraints, and medication, and you can't handle her. Obviously she's still dangerous and violent. But you want us to take her home to our house. You're crazier than she is!"

Natalie and Brady O'Mara, about Maureen, fourteen when placed, now twenty-seven.

A responsible hospital would not recommend residential care for a child who belonged at home. Some children can be maintained at home for a brief period of time, but once the child is no longer in the hospital the pressure is off the system to find a bed in a treatment facility. The next available bed will be given to the child whose need most pressures the system, not to the child being temporarily maintained at home. In cases such as David's, where the safety of other children in the family and the neighborhood is at stake, it is important for parents to hold their ground, to hold the system accountable. In doing this the involvement of the courts is essential. This is why charges need to be pressed.

This chapter will end with Joseph, because in his story you will see the courtship of parents with an unattached child whose hunger for nurturing cannot be satisfied in its sexual aspects. The lack of sexual nurture frustrates Joseph, increasing his rage, while his response to appropriate nurture forges his parents' bonding to him. Herein lies the poignancy of life in some adoptive families—the daily weaving of heartwarming and chilling interactions that keep hope in constant counterpoint with fear.

❧ We got Joseph when he was four years old. He had been born to a fifteen year old, lived with her in foster care, and was carried by her from motel to truck stop when she was prostituting. But we didn't know all this. We fell in love with him when we met him one Saturday, and the social worker delivered him to us the following Tuesday with a box containing everything he owned. At a shower a friend had given me some Levis and a flannel shirt for him. He put them on and came flying out the door saying, "Daddy, here comes your mountain boy." That was one of the wonderful moments that balances the others.

Joseph felt abandoned, and there was nothing we could do to compensate. He had crying rages. On the morning of his fourth day with us, he was playing on the bed. I wanted to make the bed before taking a shower and getting dressed, but he wouldn't gather up his toys. "Mommies don't get dressed. They go in the shower then get in bed naked with me, and this is what we do." I explained that this mother didn't do that. We had no preparation for this, and it was really hard to wing it and hope we were saying the right things. He had been accustomed to sexual nurturing, which I wouldn't do. That, and the feeling of abandonment made him very angry.

At first it was easy to rock and console him, but the longer this went on, the more frustrated we got. My husband would come home and I'd leave. Joseph hadn't been here very long when he locked his heels into the kitchen floor and told me to get fucked. Being rescuers, and wanting very much to love this child, we ignored it.

Joseph would tell us about his nightmares, but he wouldn't tell us about his feelings, so at breakfast one morning I sang to him my feelings. He then sang his to me, and that's when the really good times when we were able to connect began. We sang in the car; we sang all the time. I went to Europe shortly after that. "Who's going to sing to me?" he asked. I took my tape recorder with me and kept singing to him and telling him stories about all I was seeing, then mailed him the tapes.

I made a tiny hat and smock for my thumb, Thumbelina. Thumbelina only came out when he behaved; using her I told him stories about love and family. There were tender moments and times when we felt he had bonded.

By the time Joseph was five we had him in therapy. The first therapist we took him to was a Freudian who had no trouble blaming mom. At one session she told him she was going to get rid of the bad boy. Joseph was terrified that she was going to cut out his bad part. It took me forever to convince him that I was not going to let that happen. He had to behave, but I wasn't going to let her do that because I wanted all of him.

When my daughter was little we had a tune we would whistle to each other as she came through the woods from school. Joseph said, "You don't do that for me," so I started doing it and he would whistle his way to the front door.

My daughter was very active in theater and ballet, and Joseph wanted a special activity of his own. He wanted to read. He had just started kindergarten but was not happy because they had not promised to teach him to read. While my daughter was at dance class, I read to Joseph, pointing out the words and syllables as I read them. After I had read the book to him several times, he read it to me. That night he read to his dad from an article about MX missiles. He's very bright, a natural reader.

We went to another therapist, and another. We were told we didn't love him enough, that we made a distinction because he was adopted, that I was overpowering and domineering. Joseph got worse.

When Joseph was eight he was going through my craft stuff and found Thumbelina's hat.

"Who really is Thumbelina?" he asked.

"I think you know, don't you? How do you feel about that?"

"I still want to believe."

One time when I was upstairs, the light fixture in the bathroom fell and broke. Joseph thought I'd hurt myself. He was not allowed upstairs, but he flew up anyway. "Are you hurt? What's happened?"

There were astonishing signs of care, and yet at other times he would threaten to kill me. I kept thinking my husband was going to come home and find me dead. Everyone I talked to about it kept saying, "What have you done to make him like that? He's only eleven."

"I think Joseph is too preoccupied with himself and masturbating too much," I said to Joseph's therapist one day.

"Have you seen it?"

"No, but he is in his room a lot and he's destroying it, spitting on the ceiling, making it a shambles, and I can't handle that."

"You just don't know how to raise a boy. Boys will be boys. They do territorial things."

"Like pee in the corner to mark their spot?"

"They've been known to do that."

"That is unacceptable in my house. I won't live like that."

"Well, you don't know how to raise a son."

No one could accept the fact that Joseph had some responsibility for the situation. Joseph held out the whole time. He didn't want anybody close.

Joseph was getting big enough to hurt me, but my husband still didn't want to believe it. It wasn't until he wasn't supposed to be here and was, and saw Joseph do some of the stuff, that it really began to dawn on him. Finally I said, "Hey, you make a choice. It's him or me." We found a home where Joseph could go temporarily to give us respite. My husband and I had been married twenty-seven years. He had always been supportive of me, but we really had to help each other through this situation with Joseph. Our goal had to be us, not him.

The woman in the respite-care home cleaned Joseph's room one day and found women's undergarments—some of mine, his sister's, and the other girls who had been in the house. He had earned three weekends home and had returned with these things. We had finally found him an attachment therapist, but it was too late. During a rage reduction therapy session Joseph admitted taking the underwear. The therapist went after him, "That's what you really wanted to do to your mom? Am I right? Am I right?" He pushed Joseph until he broke. To us he said, "You guys really handled that well. You stood up through it and did the right thing."

On the way home I told Robert, "They have no idea how angry I am. I didn't want to sit there and listen to Joseph. I wanted to tear him apart. I'm going back tomorrow and tell him." We had rage reduction therapy from Monday to Friday three or four hours a day. On Thursday, Joseph disclosed that he had molested a younger child. I told the district attorney that I wanted him arrested, and that we would refuse custody of him. I will never forget when they put the handcuffs on him. I thought I would suffocate.

So many people want to make us sorry we adopted Joseph. My husband's parents didn't want us to adopt and give him the family name. Family members commented, "You're not doing right by this kid. There's something wrong with you if you can't get your child to behave." It was one kick in the stomach after the other. When Joseph was arrested, we heard in many veiled ways that we had brought this on ourselves.

I said, "If we hadn't adopted Joseph we wouldn't have given the love that we're all supposed to give when we walked this path. We're all supposed to give back in some form or another. Yes, I hurt, but I also know that he might not be alive today if we hadn't taken him, and I have the utter joy of knowing that in spite of everything that happened to him, Joseph knows that he was loved." His unhappiness, dysfunction, sickness, won't take the good times away. The wonderful times when we connected made him my son.

Joseph and I were meant to be together. When I was eight months pregnant with my daughter, I had a dream that I was pregnant with a little girl. About two weeks later I had a dream about a little boy with brown hair whose name was Joseph. When we decided to adopt, and the social worker called and said, "I have a kid I want you to come in and look at. His name is Joseph," we knew we were supposed to have him. I've grown from what I learned from his goodness, and what I have learned from his pain.

Georgia Mack, about Joseph, four when placed, sixteen now. The Macks also have a birth child.

6

The Child with Provocative Behavior

The purpose of provocative behavior is to get a reaction by inciting someone to do or feel something. One way children take control is by pushing parent's buttons. In the heat of the moment it is very difficult not to react. Children who don't trust adults and are afraid of closeness distance their parents by their behavior. Children who think they are unlovable become more difficult to love; children who are angry take revenge; children who are hopeless act out their despair.

Provocative behavior can be a way for children to ask for help without the risk of being vulnerable. To get this message parents need to short circuit their reactions. Learning to do this is the greatest challenge of adoptive parenting. It requires not taking the children's behavior personally, and at the same time finding ways to contain the behavior while looking for what the child is trying to accomplish by it. The behaviors listed below are not peculiar to adopted children except perhaps in their prevalence and degree of seriousness.

Stealing

Because "thou shall not steal" is one of the commandments, stealing is often looked upon as a sin rather than just an acting-out behavior. And it assumes the adopted child has been brought up in a religious household or at least one in which other people's things were respected. This is rarely the case in older child adoptions. The challenge for adoptive parents is not to react out of their own value system but to treat stealing like any other unacceptable behavior that needs to be eliminated. Sometimes stealing can be dealt with by removing the temptation.

❧ I knew Sandy would steal. It went on for maybe a year. I didn't talk about it. I just took my money with me wherever I went. Later Sandy admitted, "Yeah, I used to steal." But we never got into how much it happened because it wasn't enough to disrupt the household.

Ellen Valdez, single parent of Sandy, twelve when placed, seventeen now.

Adoptive parents need to take control more than other parents, and they need to gather information beyond what the child is willing to give because they cannot assume the child has the expected inner controls. For a parent who respects personal privacy, it feels wrong to search a child's room. But often it is essential, because it can reveal problems that need to be dealt with. Trust is something that must be earned.

❧ We made the mistake of trusting them around money. We discovered they had stolen from my mother-in-law, but she didn't tell us because she didn't want to embarrass us. When I was cleaning I found the money stuffed under the bed. For a couple of years our money and jewelry had to be locked up. We locked up the sugar too, because if Lucille had too much sugar she lost it.

Edsel and Marcia Dean, about Kerry, Lucille, and Clayton, five, eight, and four when placed separately, eighteen, fourteen, and twelve now.

Another parent responded to the behavior by giving her child the experience of what it felt like to be stolen from.

❧ Occasionally I miss a piece of jewelry and find it in Leslie's pocket. Then I either borrow something of hers without asking or I fine her. Leslie will not give up a penny; she is Jack Benny reincarnated. If I fine her it breaks her heart.

Thelma and Mark Irwin, about Leslie, four when placed, eight now.

For most children, developing a conscience appropriate to their age is a major part of the solution, the younger and sooner the better. For some, particularly older children, their own needs remain paramount; then the stealing becomes more serious.

🌶 Linda stole five hundred dollars a day for five days within a two-week period of time. Then she ran away. The next day she came home, and the guidance counselor called to find out if she was here. He had heard from another student that Linda had talked about running away.

"As a matter of fact," he said, "I think you should check your wallet to see if your bank card is missing. Linda has had a great deal of money and has purchased gold chains for some boys."

I woke Linda up and asked where my bank card was. She was groggy enough to say, "It's over there on the shelf."

When she got up she wanted to talk to her therapist and go to the hospital. She said, "I'm never going to get better unless you let me go to a hospital."

Clearly Linda felt out of control, but her diagnosis was not severe enough to warrant hospitalization, so we started a three-times-a-week therapy program with Linda living at home. We set up ways she could earn the money to repay me with jobs around the house. For almost a month, every time I passed the bank I got nauseated.

Phyllis Tate, single parent of Linda, eleven when placed, fourteen now.

Linda's stealing took her mother to the edge of her finances. As overwhelming as this was, if the child accepts the consequences and deals with the underlying causes in therapy, the breach of trust these incidents cause can heal.

There are children who seem to have no regard for the rules of family life and who continue to inflict pain without apparent remorse. Others keep repeating their mistakes over and over even though they have been taught otherwise or suffered the consequences. Some of these children are unattached, and some are suffering from neurological damage resulting from genetics, substance abuse, and poor nutrition during pregnancy.

🌶 Last year Casey backed a truck up to the apartment and ripped me off. He took my golf clubs, VCR, credit cards. Then he went on a spending spree. I called the police. They filed a report. Nothing happened. Eventually he was put in residential care on a voluntary basis. They made him go to group the first night after supper. As soon as the lights were out that night he left. He showed up here.

I said, "They're offering you a chance to get some stuff together. Take it." He kept running away, so eventually they called and said, "He doesn't want to be here and there are kids who do, so we're discharging him." Casey came back.

"I want to be home."

"You don't live here."

"I'm discharged." He was homeless for about a week, and then he began breaking in during the day. I called the police.

"This is your own kid you've locked out. What do you want us to do?"

"Something!"

It wasn't that I needed an order of protection, but my stuff did. One night hearing my own car start woke me up. Casey drove around all night and returned about five in the morning. I went to the police station to report the theft, but they wouldn't file it because it was my own son and the car wasn't gone twenty-four hours. I got a car lock.

"I can't keep you out since you've broken all the windows, so you might as well come in." It was hopeless. I looked at the calendar. Only 365 days until he's eighteen. I can make it.

Casey started talking about making restitution. I told him, "In taking my things, what you stole from me is trust. You've got a year for restitution. If that's not important to you, when you're eighteen, you're out. If you come back because you need a place to stay, sorry."

One day I got a call from the credit-card company telling me that somebody was trying to buy four leather jackets on my credit card. I asked Casey about it. I wanted to trust him. "Oh, Father, you must have dropped it someplace. You have to believe me this time. I didn't do it. I have a job interview now, will you drive me?" I did.

When I got home the phone rang. It was the police. Casey had been caught in the mall with two thousand dollars worth of merchandise and my credit card. They confiscated the card for evidence and asked me, "Will you be taking him?"

"No, you take him."

Within two hours he was home.

Some days I'd say, "Let's have supper together. Do you want to cook or wash the dishes?

"Neither."

As he got close to being eighteen, I just stopped trying. He'd come home and say, "What's for supper?"

"I stopped and ate on my way home."

"What am I going to eat? There's no food in the cupboard."

"If you're not going to help out, and every time I leave you alone you rip me off, why should I keep the cupboard stocked?"

He was arrested for shoplifting, and the police called, "Come and get him."

"I'm not going to."

"We will file charges against you for abandonment."

Can you imagine what that would look like on my record if I wanted to study social work? Or wanted to get another kid? I picked him up. He likes over-the-counter drugs and had been found looking for his locker, disoriented because he had shoplifted and taken dramamine. After that, he was gone two or three days out of the week.

When he was eighteen I said, "Spread your wings. Go run your own program." Soon he was asking to move back in.

"It's real hard."

"I'm sure it is, and I'm sure you'll figure it out and survive." Later, when he got evicted, he came back again, "All I need is a place to sleep."

"You've got it. There's the park."

"Can I come back and just sleep on the couch?"

"You can sleep in a sleeping bag outside."

"What would I have to do to come back in?"

"I want my VCR and golf clubs back, my calculators, change, and everything else you took including the two thousand dollars. Trust is easily destroyed and it takes a long time to rebuild."

"Well, can we go to the movies then?"

"Sure." I probably could let him in to spend the night and he probably wouldn't rip me off, but it's more important for me to tell him that he really ruined this and if he wants to come back he'll have to work real hard.

Earl Raleigh, single parent of Casey, thirteen when placed, eighteen now.

The ingratiating "Well, can we go to the movies then?" makes the parent feel wanted and hooked into the relationship. It is this push-pull dynamic that alternately destroys and resurrects hope; it makes adoptive parenting like an emotional roller-coaster ride. Carried to the extreme, as with Casey, it feels crazy, like something is disconnected.

One of the effects of fetal alcohol syndrome is brain damage disconnecting the cause-and-effect mechanisms. Casey's birth dad was schizophrenic, so Casey's genetics weren't good, and there was a history of substance abuse in his birth mother's family, so the probability of damage in utero was high. This, combined with his early negative experiences and resultant serious emotional damage, created a lethal mix.

In the samples discussed in this book alone there are four other adoptions with similar outcomes to Casey's. Would a less damaged child have been able to make better use of this adoptive home? Have Casey's chances of living a happy, productive life been increased at all by his adoption? Would a therapeutic, highly structured group home have provided Casey with better socialization? In permanency planning, should we triage on the basis of both genetics and history? Is every child adoptable? Is it enough that this adoption did not disrupt? What kept this single parent from disrupting this adoption—from ending his paternal relationship with Casey emotionally and legally?

❧ The thing about Casey that kept me going was that there wasn't any malice and we had good times. We traded books. We both like to cook. Sometimes he was the white knight who was going to right the wrongs of the world. But he did hurt animals, and to this day he likes fire. He ripped me off but wouldn't allow anybody else to try it. If I called he would come to my aid. But I wanted to be Dad, and Casey couldn't give what I expected, so I had to push that fantasy aside.

Now I still have a son and a sense that "I did it." The future for Casey is not as bleak as I thought. He's a hustler and quite articulate. He can always find a job, but he has a hard time keeping it. He does best at temp work—two or three days and he moves on. He might just make it, and that feels good.

Earl Raleigh, single parent of Casey, thirteen when placed, eighteen now.

In spite of everything, Casey was able to give enough back and his dad was willing to let go of enough expectations that they stayed together. To some degree these are the ingredients of every older child adoption that does not disrupt. The question remains, however: In cases like Casey's, is this enough?

Lying

Most children lie to keep from getting in trouble. Some can't tell the difference between what is true and what they wish were true. Some, like Libby, lie for no apparent reason. Depending on the cause, this can be confabulation or crazy lying. Some people confabulate when they don't remember the facts; they make something up to fill in the gaps. In some cases the memory loss has been caused by neurological damage resulting from the mother's alcohol or drug consumption during pregnancy. Libby's lying, for example, could be confabulation.

❧ Libby was slippery; she lied a lot. One day when she came home from school she pulled a folder I didn't recognize out of her backpack.

"Where did this come from?" I asked.

She told me a long, involved story about how a girl in her home state had given it to her and Libby had brought it with her. Inside the cover was the name and address of a girl in school here. I called her, because I thought Libby had stolen the notebook. She had stolen things before.

The girl said, "Libby liked it because it has a unicorn on it, so I gave it to her. She's my best friend."

I asked Libby why she had made up the story. She said, "I don't know. It seemed like a good idea at the time."

The last time I took her to confession she told the priest, "I lie because it's easier sometimes and if I get away with it I don't get into trouble."

She tried to get me to agree that she wouldn't get into trouble if she told the truth, but I said, "I can say that your trouble is going to be less if you don't lie, but I can't guarantee that you're not going to get a lecture or that nothing's going to happen to you because of what you did."

Thelma and Mark Irwin, about Libby, four when placed, eight now.

If Libby's problem had been crazy lying, which occurs in some attachment disordered children, she might be caught pulling the folder out of her friend's book bag and, when asked what she was doing with the folder, respond, "What folder?"

The difficulty some adopted children have in separating fact from fiction becomes very serious when some therapists want to work with the kids alone. When a child spins a story that denigrates their adoptive parents or even fabricates abuse, the therapist may believe the child is being victimized. This elicits sympathy in the therapist for the child and moves the focus from helping the child with his or her problems to "fixing" the parents. It may even result in the parents being reported for abuse.

> ✿   Leslie could win an academy award. She tells the story the way she wishes it were. Even if she's not doing it deliberately, she needs someone next to her saying, "It didn't happen that way."
>   *Thelma and Mark Irwin, about Leslie, four when placed, eight now.*

Running Away

Running away is worrisome behavior for parents. Where is she? Is he all right? If parents don't know where their child is, they can hardly keep the child safe. There is a sense of helplessness. The seriousness of run-away behavior can be measured by the length of time the children are gone. Most children are gone for several hours, a few overnight. When children are young or run away early in the placement, it is important to go after them.

> ✿   Lucille was in pre-adoptive placement with another family in town. I had seen her picture on the bulletin board at Social Services and commented, "She's cute."
>   "Not!" said the social worker standing next to me. "She has lots of problems."
>   Lucille had threatened the family with a knife, and they had called Social Services to have her removed. She was in second grade and was put in a pre-adolescent treatment center just before Christmas. Social Services asked us to take her without telling us about the knife incident.

There was a lot of antagonism over discipline. At night we locked all family members' doors so they could get out, but she couldn't get in. At Christmas we bought everyone an equal number of presents. Lucille announced, "I'm running away." The boys helped her out the door with her toys. She looked like a homeless person. When she didn't come right back, we went to get her. She was on route 35 waiting to be picked up.

"Lucille, get in the car," I said.

When we got home she went up to her room.

Edsel and Marcia Dean, about Lucille, eight when placed, fourteen now.

Later in placement with an older child it is important to figure out whether the child wants attention or needs time-out—and act accordingly. Calvin wanted attention. Running away is a dangerous way to get attention, so it is best not to reward it.

🐦 "I'm going to run away," Calvin announced one evening.

"OK," I said. He stomped around, packed, slammed the door a few times. Finally, he went by me, his pack stuffed, his socks hanging out. He didn't look back, just slammed the door. I was sitting there drinking coffee.

About an hour and a half later I got a phone call. "Come pick me up."

"Where?"

"The county jail."

"You made good time."

"I'm not at the police station."

"Where are you?"

"The mall. Be careful when you back up the car. I put my knapsack under it so it wouldn't get wet."

I had read that one reasonably well.

Milton Yardley, single parent of Calvin, thirteen when placed, twenty-one now.

Sometimes Andy used running away to get what he wanted; sometimes he just needed time out.

🐦 Andy's birth father was much older than his mother and had adult children from a former marriage. His mother would drop him off with any of these adult half brothers and sisters who would take him for a period of time so she could get a break. There was little consistency in his early life, so a lot of nurturing steps were missed. He needs a lot of reassurance, so he is testing all the time. "I'm going to run away." "I'm going to kill myself." We have to ask ourselves to see if he is testing to see what we are going to do or if he's really in crisis.

The last time it happened it was a control thing. My wife and I had plans that night, and he didn't want us to leave.

"I'm going to go in the middle of the night."

"You're not going to pack a bunch of stuff now and leave in a couple of hours. You're going to leave now."

I took him outside and said, "OK, take off."

He walked, turtle speed, to the field directly opposite our house where we could watch him the whole time. He was back in half an hour.

At other times there is no reasoning with him, so we have signed a contract in therapy that if he needs to run away there is a specific place in the yard where he can go and we will not bother him. We'll just check every half an hour to see that he is there. He, in turn, has promised not to hurt himself. He usually needs that kind of space when he is in trouble, when his anxiety has gotten him all worked up about everybody hating him, or when he's gotten into so much trouble that he feels unable to stand it and thinks he might as well kill himself or run away. We are helping him see choices other than running, like using his punching bag or doing the job he forgot to do.

Gail and Hector Garrett, about Andy, seven when placed, thirteen now.

Threatening Suicide

Suicide is a permanent form of running away. It can be a threat that is a louder cry for help from a child whose feeling of desperation is becoming intolerable. The older the child, the more serious the threat. Adolescence is a particularly vulnerable time, especially for adoptees. Adoptive parents walk a tightrope in dealing with this because of the serious consequences of overreacting and underreacting.

Younger children don't understand the seriousness of suicide; they can think of suicide and running away as synonymous. For them it might be a way of asking, "Do you love me?"

Some parents use humor to diffuse the situation, because when the behavior does not get the desired rise out of the parent, it stops.

🌲 Kerry did some real acting out. I remember him holding a knife to his throat and saying, "I'm going to kill myself, Ma. What do you think? Would it bother you?"

"I don't know, Kerry. It depends on how much blood you get on the floor, whether you rip the wall." I took it lightly right away, but it was scary.

Edsel and Marcia Dean, about Kerry, five when placed, eighteen now.

In school or anywhere Lucille will call me just about anything. She can really get me going. Punishing her is more to get it out of my system, it doesn't do anything to her. Last week she wouldn't study for her exams no matter what I did, and she got very abusive. It escalated to, "Don't come to my graduation. I'm not going to my graduation. I'm going to jump off the roof."

Lately she says things like that. Sometimes I joke with her. "From what part, Lucille, the high roof or the deck?"

This goes on for a couple of hours, maybe overnight, and then the sun comes out. They had a terrible time getting her to stand and walk straight for graduation, but she made it.

Edsel and Marcia Dean, about Lucille, eight when placed, fourteen now.

Having a therapist to help you assess these situations is essential. Lucille was in therapy, but therapists familiar with adoption issues are hard to find.

🌲 Dolores came in November. A month later we went back to the foster family for a Christmas visit because they had adopted her brothers and we had agreed to keep in touch. We exchanged gifts and had a really nice day. After that Dolores began to deteriorate rapidly. She became very brittle. By the middle of January I was frantic trying to find a therapist. I called those who were recommended, but most indicated that I must be causing the problem and that made no sense to me. I had only been Dolores's mother for two months.

Then one day Dolores went to school with six band-aids on her face covering self-inflicted scratches. I called the social worker, "We have to have a therapist today." She had just heard of one who specialized in adoption and he agreed to see us that afternoon.

When we arrived the therapist was standing at the top of the steps with a benign smile. Dolores stomped angrily up the steps yelling, "I don't know why you're taking me to this place." We went into the counseling room, sat down, and the therapist leaned forward and said quietly,

"So why'd you kill your mother?"

"I didn't."

"That's right, you didn't. So why are you acting like this?"

I was shocked by this way of beginning. I thought it would only make her worse. But I had no options. As I watched, Dolores began to relax. She became less brittle every day. The hostility kept coming, but the therapist helped me to see that it wasn't me she was really angry at, so I didn't take it personally and could keep holding on.

Hope Walker, single parent of Dolores, twelve when placed, eighteen now.

Suicide threats take adoptive parents to the edge because both hospitalizing and not hospitalizing the child have serious consequences for the relationship. Hospitalizing can be interpreted by the child as another rejection, but certainly it is better to err on the side of safety and have the consequences to live with. Hospitalization is not something that "cures" suicidal behavior or other serious problems. It is an opportunity for the child—and the family—to have a break. The hospital can provide a safe, controlled atmosphere and professionals trained to help diagnose and temporarily stabilize potentially dangerous behaviors. If hospital staff is knowledgeable about adoption and other related issues, the hospitalization can be a starting point for important work.

Succeeding in Failing

Most people want to succeed. Failure may result from attempting a task beyond one's strength, laziness, not completing a task, or unforeseen circumstances. Children who are so lacking in a sense of self-worth that they don't feel they deserve positive rewards will jeopardize themselves so that they do not succeed. If you're a parent who helps your child because you assume, like most people, that the child wants to succeed, his or her refusal can be mystifying.

🌸 One time when Mitchell was in high school he did a report that looked like a fifth grader had done it. I said, "Oh, Mitchell, let's think of another way to do it."

We brain-stormed, he got all excited, and did a wonderful project. I thought he felt really good about himself. He got a zero.

"What happened?" I asked.

"The teacher wasn't there when I went to hand it in, so I left it in the classroom. When I went back to get it, it wasn't there."

"Did you tell the teacher you had done it?"

"No."

His story didn't make sense, and all I could think of was that he couldn't allow himself to succeed. I don't know how to fight that. We thought that if we believed in him, supported him, he would get some confidence. We have worked with kids, and those who have success turn around. But it felt as if it was too scary for him to succeed, too scary for him to get close to us.

Ginger Lancaster, about Mitchell, twelve when placed, fifteen now.

🌸 My daughter was passing everything but math, so I got her a tutor. They met every Friday, and Clara went into the final exam with a B average. She failed the course. It felt like a defiant act; "You can't make me succeed." I had to let those feelings go, step back, and realize that I couldn't get for her what she didn't want for herself.

Hope Walker, single parent of Clara, thirteen when placed, eighteen now.

Wetting and Soiling

When children who are no longer toddlers come to live in a family, it is normal to expect that they have been toilet trained. This is not necessarily the case. Toilet training requires that the parent attend to the comfort of the child so that the child learns to pay attention to his or her body. Thus children learn what a full bladder or bowel feels like, and how to relieve themselves. In a neglectful family, this does not always happen; in an abusive family, mentioning discomfort often leads to more pain.

🖋 The adoption worker didn't tell me that Theo had cerebral palsy, can't talk, and poops in his pants a lot. When he first came he was eight. He'd come in from play, and there was all this BM he hadn't even noticed! It took months and months and I tried not to get mad. "Don't you smell that, Theo? Doesn't it feel uncomfortable?" Now when anything comes out, he rushes to the bathroom and washes his pants out.

Shirley Newman, about Theo, eight when placed, nine now.

There can be emotional as well as physical reasons for this condition. Sometimes sexually abused children will have damaged sphincter muscles or will have blocked out the feeling from that part of the body to defend against pain. Angry children become constipated, but stain can leak around the blocked stool.

🖋 Millie lived with her birth parents until she was four or five. Then she lived in foster care. Two or three times she thought she was finally home but was moved again. Her father wouldn't release her for adoption. When she was ten she testified against her parents and their rights were terminated. Her father might still be in jail for what he did to her.

When Millie came to us she looked like a frightened animal. Her fingers were frostbitten because she had been left in a crawl space. She spoke in one-word sentences. She didn't know how to bathe, so I got in the shower with her and showed her how. She wet all the time and had terrible body odor. She didn't want to get off her roller skates to come in and go to the bathroom. I kept telling her, "If you're tired you need to take a nap, if you're hungry you need to eat, if you need to go to the bathroom you have to go. Your body is not a terrible thing. It's a gift to you and you need to take care of it."

Now she has the body of a teenager and only wets her pants or the bed when she's upset. It's my trigger to pull her aside and say, "Come on now, what is it? Wetting the bed is not acceptable at twelve, it wasn't at ten. There's got to be another way to deal with it."

Recently she wet the bed the day my parents were coming. They don't accept adopted children as their grandchildren. It's not just Millie they don't accept. My brother married a woman who already had two children and my parents don't accept them either. I told her, "Millie, I bet your birth parents didn't do everything you wanted. Well, mine don't do what I want either sometimes." Then I showed her how to do the laundry and we made the bed.

Angela Jackson, about Millie, ten when placed, twelve now.

Bed wetting can be an unconscious reaction to anxiety or the result of sleeping so deeply that the full bladder does not sound a loud enough internal alarm. Whatever the reason, it is important to work cooperatively with the child to eliminate the behavior.

🐚 Kelly used to wet the bed, then make it. She'd put her wet pajamas under the bed with all her clothes. After getting caught at that she started putting her pajamas under her pillow. Finally I said, "Look, the washing machine's here. All you have to do is take everything off the bed and put it in the washing machine." I showed her how to start it. "This is all you have to do. I will not yell at you. I understand."

She did well, except when she went pooh, she wrapped it all inside and put it into the washing machine with her clothes.

One day Kelly took the top of the stack of clean towels off, went pooh, and put the clean towels back on top of it all. Every time we took a shower we took a towel to dry ourselves. Her sister said, "Ma, look at this." She had gotten out of the shower, reached for the towel with her eyes shut, and it was all over her.

Clyde and Julia Edwards, about Kelly, eight when placed, twelve now.

The more pain a child has inside, the greater his or her acting out will be. Unfortunately, believing and remembering this doesn't make it easy to live with children who go to the bathroom anywhere—and know better.

> ❧ One day when I went into the living room where Darcy was watching TV, I smelled urine.
>
> "Darcy, did you wet your pants?" (He still wets the bed sometimes.)
>
> "No. I think the cat might have peed on the rug."
>
> Darcy had peed over one corner of the living room and the couch. "I was watching TV and I didn't want to miss my show to get up and go the bathroom."
>
> I made him clean it up, scrub the rug and couch, but when he went to bed I had to redo it because he didn't get all the smell out. When he has to clean up after himself he doesn't do it again for a while. Everything works temporarily, but only temporarily.
>
> *Ida Aldez, single parent of Darcy, two when placed, eight now.*

Splitting

Splitting means separating two elements that ought to go together. It can happen in the child's thought processes or can be created in the child's environment. Splitting inside the child's thought processes can affect bonding and identity formation. Exterior splitting is a way the child can manipulate those around him.

All children at some point in their development think in terms of the good parent and the bad parent—the one who takes them to the circus and the one who expects them to clean their room. For most children this is the same parent, and in time they understand there are different aspects to everyone, including themselves, so the split in their thinking heals. For adopted children it is more complicated. Since they have two sets of parents, they can think of the parents they are living with as the bad parents who discipline them and fantasize their birth parents as people who would give them everything they want.

This kind of split thinking stalls the bonding process and complicates identity formation. Most children adopted when they are older were taken out of abusive, dysfunctional families. Am I like my birth parent? Like my adoptive parent? Who am I? The process of putting together the genetic and environmental elements of personality formation is much more complicated for the adopted child.

🌢 Rosa said to me once, "You know I've really come a long way. I'm eighteen, I don't have any kids, and I'm still in school. I'm a success. I'm like a raging success, and people still want more from me. When is it going to end? Don't you see how far I've come?"

"You're right. You're way past your birth mom. You would have had two or three kids by now and not be in school."

"I know if I'd stayed in that situation I wouldn't be where I am today."

Rosa has another year of high school, and she's talking about college. She doesn't want to go away to school, so she's looking for a college where she can commute. Once you get the sex thing out of the way with kids, whatever age that comes, then you don't have to be so parental anymore. You can relax and let them be, because they're not going to be the same as you are no matter where they came from. It's frightening, but after a while they show you that they're not going to do anything terrible and you can sit back and enjoy what they come up with.

Elizabeth Packard, about Rosa, eleven when placed, eighteen now.

Curtis made a different choice than Rosa.

🌢 Curtis had been physically and sexually abused by both birth parents until the age of six. By the age of twelve he was a sexual perpetrator with at least four victims.

After four and a half years of treatment, during which he had two prolonged periods of progress followed by disintegration, he announced, "I'd rather leave treatment, finish my time in jail, and return to my birth parents."

He had been living for eight years split between families, unable to integrate the experience. The part of him that talked to owls, loved to go fishing, and was fascinated by Egypt was eclipsed by the rageful, hurtful, sexually internalized birth parent.

Hope Walker, single parent of Curtis, nine when placed, twelve now.

Divide and conquer is the name of the external splitting game children play. Divide Mom from Dad, siblings from parents, parents from educators. If the child wins, everyone loses. The parents no longer have control, and the splitting child no longer feels safe. Communication is essential.

🖐 Andy can't play us against each other because we are determined to be together, no matter what. It's inconvenient, but we always check with each other if we hear, "Dad said . . . " or "Mom said. . . . " That cuts out the middle play. We try to be consistent, but we don't always see the situation the same way. Sometimes we're in a struggle and trying to decide: Does he need a hug? To be left alone? To sit in his chair? What is the goal? At times I'll say, "Don't ask him what happened, he's just starting to calm down. I'll tell you in a minute." At other times my wife will say, "He's manipulating you. You shouldn't give in to him," and I respond, "No, I think he needs a hug this time." We agree to disagree, and the person who's involved sees the situation to the conclusion he or she chooses, with the support of the other. Andy's behaviors come out often enough that we'll have a chance to do it the other way and see if it works. It's a big experiment, trial and error.

   Gail and Hector Garrett, about Andy, seven when placed, thirteen now.

Sometimes the splitting behaviors are more subtle, and it takes a while to catch on. For a while Jared and Barry were in the same unit of a psychiatric hospital.

🖐 The therapist at the hospital said, "You have to present a united front." My husband and I had been married for eleven years before the boys came. We could finish each other's sentences. Now they were coming out wrong. If my husband and I were in the room with either of the boys, one of us would feel like the center of the universe, the other would feel sick.

   Mom: When we went to the hospital I sat cuddling Barry. I didn't realize that my husband was feeling left out, that Barry was pushing him away with every look.

   Dad: It looked as if everything was wonderful with Barry and my wife. I thought I shouldn't interfere.

Mom: I thought my husband was being cold, and if he were only more flexible everything would be OK. Jared was giving my husband all the wonderful feelings that Barry had been giving me. Even though I felt hurt, I thought, at least he's getting something good back from Jared.

That's how Barry and Jared split the family, carving it up the way they wanted it. I think they had decided that they couldn't both be loved by the same parent, so they would each have one. Once we got through the pain, my husband suggested a plan of action. "Today Barry's going to sit on my lap, and I'll let you know when I'm feeling good enough that he can go sit with you, or we can play a game together. The first day he was doing all the wonderful warm things with Barry, and Barry was kicking and screaming, trying to come to me. We did the reverse with Jared. Now they both have both parents.

Craig and Mitzi Clark, about Barry and Jared, three and four when placed, eleven and twelve now.

When the parents do not present a united front, splitting can cost the placement and even the marriage.

❧ When Jess reached seventh grade he became verbally abusive to me, manipulative with my husband and me, and the subject of a call from the school every day. When Jess screwed up he got my husband's undivided attention. He spent hours pleading and lecturing. "I'll never give up on Jess," he said. Jess would get to him, but he'd get over it. Sometimes my husband would even ask me, "What did you do to set him off?"

I had done the nurturing for the first five years. I was so weary I felt as if I were in a pit being buried alive. By the middle of the second semester of Jess's seventh-grade year I wasn't eating or sleeping and I vomited a lot. I couldn't deal with it anymore. We had become a dysfunctional family, screaming and fighting all the time. Finally I said to my husband, "You're the father, you want Jess desperately, you're going to have to give me a break." I focused on giving our girls the support they needed, clinging to them because they are very nurturing kids. The support of my friends and daughters was my sanity.

Finally, at the end of that school year, the social worker told my husband, "If you don't get Jess out of your home, at least for a little while, you're not going to have a family." Jess was told, "Mom is not handling things with you right now. We have to give her a chance to be away from you, and you have to get your act together, so we're sending you to a place where you can." My husband likes being the good guy and making me the bad guy.

One of the most threatening things in my marriage was that I was being judged about my lack of caring for this kid who had destroyed our house, burned the neighbor's house, abused their horses, and verbally abused me. When Jess called from the treatment facility, my husband rated me as to how caring my end of the conversation was.

"You're not helping."

"Don't you judge me. I've done my best."

By that time we were in marital therapy. The therapist asked, "Why did you allow Jess to emotionally abuse your wife? You have to protect your wife and daughters first and Jess last." My husband began to realize that to have a son he has to have an intact family, and I think he enjoyed his family life while Jess was gone. Our daughters are super kids, we weren't screaming at each other, and we didn't have Jess coming between us. He was gone for a year, and during that time I became the strong person I was before. When Jess came home he knew this was his last chance, so he worked very hard.

Last week we had an incident where Jess was supposed to be home at 9 o'clock and came home at 10:30. If Jess had stuck with the truth—they were with the other kid's dad and ran out of gas— it would have been OK. But he came in defensive, nasty mouthed, belligerent. My husband said, "If you don't want to live by our rules, you're gone." I needed to hear that. Jess was horrible the next morning, and I stood tall.

"You start getting out of hand and we're contacting your probation officer."

"I think I'd rather go to jail."

When he came home from school he gave me a big hug. "I've been a jerk. I treated you horribly, and I'm really sorry. I had no right to talk to you that way."

"Jess, you know I have high hopes for you, and it broke my heart when you acted so horrible to me because if I give up, you're gone." It snowed that night, and the next day he was out shoveling the deck and the driveway without being asked.

My husband wanted a son. Jess lived in our home, but he wasn't a son. We gave up on Jess being a son and took what we could get. We don't have to have Jess nurture us. We get our support elsewhere.

Kim Brown, about Jess, nine when placed, thirteen now.

Not only do parents need to work together, but professionals need to work with and respect them as part of the treatment team. If they don't, the child can set them up against each other, become the victim, and avoid responsibility. Older children in adoption or foster care often become very skilled at being professional victims and reaping the benefits. Feeling sorry for a child and blaming someone else for the child's misbehavior is a symptom of having been duped. The child has succeeded in splitting the professionals, or, as happens more often, the professionals and the family.

✎ Jared stopped working in family therapy and in school. We didn't understand what was happening until we were called to a meeting with the school psychologist. She told us how appalled she was at the way we were treating Jared. This was our introduction to how Jared manipulates and how psychologists can be taken in.

Jared had hooked the school psychologist into concentrating on changing our behavior rather than responding to his. Group counseling with the other kids in his class was on his Individual Education Plan (IEP), but individual therapy was not. Regardless, he was being sent to the school psychologist. We confronted Jared about his manipulative behavior. Then we called the school district and psychologist to remind them that they were not authorized to provide individual therapy because Jared has that privately. The power link was broken, so Jared began working in school and behaving at home again.

Craig and Mitzi Clark, about Jared, four when placed, twelve now.

Reporting Parents to Child Protective Services

Every parent has a bottom line in terms of intolerable behavior. "I can take a lot so long as the child tells the truth . . . doesn't steal . . . isn't cruel to animals . . . isn't promiscuous. . . . " People concentrating on being good parents don't even think about being reported to Child Protective Services. But it happens, and when it does they are devastated. And sometimes the child's behavior is so provocative that parents lose it.

✒ The summer before last Mitchell couldn't get a job and ended up hanging around home. He connected with kids up the road and stole six hundred dollars from their parents' bedroom. The next morning the mother came to the house and told us what happened. Mitchell said, "Gee I don't know anything about that." While we were talking, my husband was up searching Mitchell's room. He found the six hundred dollars. We were totally embarrassed and so angry with Mitchell. We brought Mitchell to their house, because it was the husband's money. He told Mitchell how hard he had worked to save that money, which was to buy a new front door. Mitchell never said he was sorry. We asked the guy to press charges, but he refused. Mitchell's counselor said, "Call those people and tell them that the worst thing they can do is not report it to the police." We did, and Mitchell had to go to court and was put on probation.

Sometime after that Mitchell wasn't home from school when I got home from work. Eventually he showed up. I thought he was on drugs because his eyes were glassed over and he was defiant, which he had never been before. He pushed all my buttons, and I yelled at him. Mitchell stormed out of the room and slammed the door. I was shaking I was so angry. My husband was upset because I was upset, so he followed Mitchell upstairs.

"Look at me when I am talking to you." Mitchell wouldn't, so my husband put his hand under his chin to raise his head. He smelled smoke.

"You've been smoking again."

"So what are you going to do about it? Fuck off!"

My husband lost it and slapped his face. Mitchell came running down the stairs with my husband running after him. Mitchell got on his bike and took off. Soon the phone rang. It was the police. Mitchell had called them to say that his father had hit him. The policeman came, we talked, and he told Mitchell he should spend the night somewhere else, so he went to his girlfriend's.

The next day we were supposed to see the probation officer. Mitchell wouldn't get in the car with my husband because he said it wasn't safe. That really hurt my husband.

"Will you go if I come with you?" I asked. So I left work, picked him up, and we were alone in the car.

"Why isn't it safe to be with Dad all of a sudden?"

"He hit me."

"Mitchell, I don't condone his hitting you, but I understand it. What would you do if your kid told you to fuck off to your face? He lost it. But you knew damn well what you were doing. You didn't come home, you were smoking, you sassed him right to his face. This part of it is your responsibility. Don't blame it all on Dad."

Shortly after that Mitchell ran away. We called everybody. Finally, after Christmas, we got an anonymous letter from his biological grandfather. Mitchell had returned to his birth mom. Three months later Mitchell's brother brought him home, sat at our kitchen table, and said, "I really thought I could help Mitchell, but I can't." A few days later Mitchell and I were sitting at the kitchen table.

"Do you know what my mother's real dream is?" he asked.

"What?"

"She wants to buy a house so we can all get back together."

"What do you think about that, Mitchell?"

"I don't think it would work, but that's what she'd like. She wants Muriel to come for a visit."

"What would you think of Muriel living down there?"

"I don't think she should go, because you've helped her more than anybody, and she needs you. My mother wouldn't do that stuff."

Muriel has lots of needs, but she gives back. She's blossomed. Everyone loves her. Mitchell's relationships don't last. He lets everybody down. He hasn't dealt with what he needs to, and he isn't going to do it until he can't get what he wants without it. My husband didn't want Mitchell to stay.

"We can't throw him out in the street."

"He can stay long enough for us to find him another place to live."

Mitchell wouldn't go back to school. I told him, "You can't just live off of us, we're struggling as it is." Then we thought of Job Corps. That's where he is. He doesn't contact us much, but he's gotten his high school equivalence, and he's learning culinary arts.

I really don't want Mitchell back home, but I want to be connected. Mitchell's not at the point where he can connect back. We thought if we just cared enough and provided a good solid home, the kids would turn around. We were naive.

Ginger Lancaster, about Mitchell, twelve when placed, fifteen now.

Sometimes when children call Child Protective Services there is no incident to be reported. There's a fabrication or a memory of prior abuse, with the child blaming the adoptive parent.

✍ Andy is good at coming up with stories that we beat him. He first did this when the girls had been here three months and the social worker came for her monthly check on them. She'd take each girl by herself, then Andy, then take them all out for ice cream and come back to talk to us. One day she said, "I need to talk to you two. Andy says a few days ago you took him in the basement, hung him from the ceiling, punched him in the stomach, back, and legs till he threw up, and left him hanging there for a while." She really believed him! We were flabbergasted.

"Come on, look at the facts. He was just out swimming with everybody. There are no marks on him."

"We have to believe the child. The girls are going to be removed and Child Protective Services is going to investigate."

"Did you talk to the girls about this? Moira's seven. What did she say?"

We talked for a while. The social worker left in the early afternoon saying, "I need to go back and talk to my supervisor."

We were shocked and really hurt. Andy was in his room crying, so when we got calm, we tried to find out what was going on,

"Andy, why are you crying?"

"I told the social worker some stories."

"What did you tell her?"

"That you tied me in the basement and hit me till I threw up."

"Did I do that to you?"

"No."

"Why did you tell her that?"

"I don't know."

"You've got to straighten this out." We got a tape recorder, but when he was talking into it he went back to his old story. We couldn't believe it.

By evening we hadn't heard anything, and the sheriff hadn't come out. It was hell. We had a baby sitter, so we went out. We tried to think why he would make this up when he wasn't even in trouble. We came home and didn't sleep much that night. In the morning I said to my wife, "Enough is enough. We are not going to live this way any more." I called the social worker and said, "If you really think that we are abusing these kids, come and get all three of them, and you better know what you are doing because there will be hell to pay. We're not going to live like this one more second. I want to know right now if you are coming to take the kids."

There was silence, then, "No, we are not coming to take the kids." We found out later that she was an inexperienced social worker who overreacted.

The incident caused her to start looking for Andy's file. We had always been told there was no background information. It took her a year to find it. Now each year when he starts school we take his file to the new teacher and explain the circumstances. "If he comes in one day and says we're beating him, don't call the sheriff and have him on our doorstep. Call his therapist or social worker. We're not going to beat him, but we understand that you can't take our word for that. Just please don't overreact." Andy knows we do this, and it has taken the wind out of his sails.

Gail and Hector Garrett, about Andy, seven when placed, thirteen now.

Being Destructive

❧ Jess was very destructive. The first week he moved in here he broke almost all my daughter's LP records over his knee. He started a fire in the closet upstairs. His favorite thing was to carve four-letter words in the windowsills. He wrote the F word everywhere. He had to sand the furniture because we were not going to be looking at four-letter words on our furniture for the rest of our lives. He stopped carving up the furniture. I got him a brand-new pair of tennis shoes. He cut a hole clear through to the bottom, wrote all over them, and that's what he wore to school. We gave him a Walkman. By the end of the week he had torn it apart and left the parts everywhere. He never knew where his bicycle was. He couldn't handle having anything good, and he didn't really care about himself or anyone else. His self-esteem was zero.

Over a year later I came home one day to find the sheriff in my driveway. Jess had abused the neighbor's horses, broken into his house with another kid, started a fire, burned all the man's important papers. The court mandated six weeks of therapy. He had been in therapy the first year, but after finalization he was no longer eligible for Medicaid, so the therapy ended. Now his case was reopened, and we were in therapy for three more years. We did holding therapy, and the therapist taught us ways to handle situations. There were automatic consequences; for example, "If you come home late, you do the dishes." I learned that I didn't create Jess, and that I had to take care of myself. If I wasn't healthy there would never be a healthy Jess.

Things worked really well until Jess hit seventh grade and stopped working in therapy. He started to just sit and look at the therapist. Finally the therapist said, "I can't do anything more with him."

Kim Brown, about Jess, nine when placed, thirteen now.

The seventh grade or age fourteen is a benchmark year for six of the boys in the sample, a large percentage for those over that age at the time of the interview. Adolescence is a difficult time for any child, but for older adopted children it is much more difficult.

Substance Abuse

Substance abuse is a behavior that provokes parents, so it is dealt with in this chapter. It differs from the other behaviors listed here in that oftentimes its purpose is not to distance the child from his parents but to distance the child from his pain. It is an anesthetic. Casey voiced this clearly.

❧ Casey's addiction was not physical. If you locked him up, he would not get the DTs. He told me he smoked dope so the rage wouldn't be so upfront. He still felt it, but he could control it. "The little things don't tick me off when I'm high. I don't get mad enough to want to break something or hurt someone."

Otherwise Casey's rage came out in property destruction or fights. He liked to destroy with knives. I'd come home and find the chairs shredded. Sometimes he'd come home with an adrenaline rush and say, "I just beat the heck out of someone. Now I can maintain for the afternoon," or, "I beat somebody up, and that's not right." There wasn't pleasure for him in hurting people. Smoking pot was like a treatment. When he was doing it, he didn't have to fight.

Earl Raleigh, single parent of Casey, thirteen when placed, eighteen now.

In addition to self-medicating, the children of substance abusers are more susceptible to becoming addicted. Since adoptive parents know very little about the circumstances of the child's time in utero, and substance abuse is one of the elements contributing to the chaos in a large percentage of homes where children are abandoned and abused, the possibility that an older adopted child will become an addict is one of the risks adoptive parents take.

Conclusion

Dealing with provocative behavior on a daily basis is difficult to endure. Eventually parents begin to feel beaten down. If needed services are not available at an affordable cost, or if the people they reach out to for help are not supportive—or worse, blaming—parents can become desperate. This puts the placement at risk. To prevent situations from deteriorating to this point two things are necessary: an adoption support group, and the availability of respite care.

Why an adoption support group? Why not just a supportive group of friends? There is a kinship born of the "We're all in this together and if you can make it I can make it, so I'm invested in your making it" mentality in an adoptive parent group.

❧ What does an adoption support group look like? A group of people sitting around talking and even laughing about the unspeakable things that have happened in their families that week without fear of being blamed or losing their right to decide the outcome. It's the Outward Bound experience with building a family out of wounded and angry children substituted for a graduated system of outdoor challenges. In the process parents learn they possess strengths they couldn't imagine needing, and they learn how to reach out to others to give and receive help.

Hope Walker, single parent of three children adopted separately.

The group is not able to change a member's reality, but any burden is easier to carry when a person does not feel alone with it. Those who have been in similar situations can share what they have learned. People who are not embroiled in a situation can often see humor in its outrageous aspects. There is nothing like laughter and camaraderie to lighten the load. In the warmth and buoyancy of such a group the most difficult challenges of life can feel like great adventures, and that feeling is energizing. It can put adoptive parents in touch with the exhilaration of the steady flow of their adrenaline and the strength they discover in themselves in the process of living their commitment to themselves and their children.

As helpful as a support group is, it only affords an hour or two of relief a week. Sometimes a longer period is needed from time to time or regularly. Why not a baby sitter? In some cases this is enough.

❧ We have had the same baby sitter for six years. She's a widow, about our age, who doesn't drive. Whenever we need baby sitting,

we drop the children off at her house. They make pizza together, do Halloween things, watch television. She's a help, and it's important to me. Even if I had more time, I don't have the energy to keep giving, giving, giving, so we need a lot of nurturing adults around to help us. I just feel like I'm not God. I can't do it all.
Edsel and Maria Dean, parents of three older children, adopted separately.

When a child is consistently difficult, eventually baby sitters refuse to come. Sometimes what parents need is a weekend or even a week to catch their breath, reconnect with each other and with their spirit of play, without breaking the bank. Such respite care cannot be done by just anyone. It needs to be someone who will provide structure similar to that provided by the child's parents—and someone who is not susceptible to the child's manipulation. It is the parents' vacation, not the child's. When effective, affordable, and loyal respite care is available, it provides parents with the relief they need to maintain their commitment to their child and to take care of themselves so that when the present difficult period is over the family will still be together.

Part 2

Living in an Adsptive Family

7

A Family that Is Different

Older child adoption isn't simply about parenting children you haven't conceived, given birth to, and brought up. It's about having a family that begins, feels, and often looks different. Birth parents can assume their children will love them and look like them; parents adopting an older child cannot. Birth parents can assume support from family members; adoptive parents cannot. But like all families, adoptive families grow individually and together in the soil of every day.

A Family that Begins Differently

The older child comes to the adoptive family not only with a different set of genes, but having had formative life experiences very different from what he or she would have had if the child been born into the adoptive family. For older children to be free for adoption, they must have lost their original family because their parents died, chose not to parent them, or neglected or abused them to the point that Child Protective Services had to intervene and place them in foster care. When children come from these situations they are as different as possible from the dimpled baby in a receiving blanket.

❧ Pamela and Wanda came in the middle of the night as foster kids when they were four and five years old. No shoes. Wanda had long hair, full of lice. Pamela's head had been shaved because of the lice, and she was wearing jeans and a T-shirt. I thought she was a boy.
Pamela threw up on a whim. If anything gagged her, she threw up. If we left the room, she threw up. She'd been left so many times she was very insecure. We just cleaned her up and reassured her as much as possible. As time went on, she adjusted.

Wanda is really strong-willed. She and her sister split a doll right down the middle once because neither one would let go. The doll got sewn up. It has turned into a positive trait for her because she knows what she wants and she'll go for it.

After five years Wanda and Pamela became available, and we adopted them. There was no way we could give them up at that point.

Carol Abbot, about Wanda, four when placed, nine now, and Pamela, five when placed, ten now.

But children aren't always adopted by their foster families. They are cared for in foster care while waiting to be reunited with their birth parents, after the birth parents have been able to rectify their situation. If the birth parents don't succeed, eventually their parental rights will be relinquished or terminated and the children will be free for adoption. This process usually takes years, during which a foster child may have the same or several moms and dads. This results in their experiencing their mom and dad as temporary figures. The "forever family" of adoption may be what adoptive parents believe they are, and what children still long for, but the children can't believe in it anymore. Parents adopting a child they have not fostered cannot assume the child will trust them. The child isn't ready to relinquish control. Such a child is wary.

🌢 We met Kerry the first time at the office of the adoption agency. He had just turned five. The agency had told us that we might want to take him out for ice cream. We were the third or fourth set of possible parents he had met. They had all taken him someplace, and he didn't want to go anywhere with us. We spent some time kidding and walking around in each other's shoes, then we got ice cream and brought it in. He ate his and said, "I want what I want, and I don't want what I don't want."

It was tough for me at first. I wanted a needy little boy who would give me a big hug. That wasn't Kerry. I had to wait four years. When we adopted Clayton I got that little boy.

Edsel and Marcia Dean, about Kerry, five when placed, eighteen now, and Clayton, four when placed, twelve now.

To adopt an older American child one has not first foster parented, approval by a licensed agency is required. This generally involves a home study, which is an assessment of the parents' needs, limits, and strengths related to parenting and adoption. Increasingly agencies and support groups are going beyond a judgmental style of report to include self-assessment tools and group preparation for parenting an older adopted child. Anecdotes describing typical older adopted child behaviors are presented to enable prospective parents to become realistic in their expectations and to focus the discussion on parenting strategies. Some candidates will be overwhelmed and drop out, some will become more realistic and look forward to the challenge, and others will imagine that after a very difficult year of adjustment to the adoption their families will live happily ever after.

A further preview into the world of older child adoption provided by some agencies is requiring the prospective parents to connect with an adoptive family who has adopted a child similar to the one they are considering. At first, prospective adoptive parents were only encouraged to visit their buddy family by agencies. Then Katherine Davis of Family Resources did a study that indicated a high correlation between adoptions which disrupted and parents who had not connected with their buddy family. Thereafter, connecting with the buddy family became a requirement for placement in that agency. It is very difficult yet absolutely essential that adoptive parents know as much as they can about what the risks and possibilities are in older child adoption. This will enable them to withdraw their application or to go forward with more realistic expectations before the child is involved. For those deciding to continue, and who do adopt, a support group is equally necessary. Having a buddy family and using a group instruction model for preparation build the foundation for the support group the parents will need after placement.

While this parent education is in process, so is the search for the child. The agency that did the home study and gave its approval of the adoptive family may have children available for adoption. Their state may have photo listings that are updated monthly; these are sometimes available in the public library. There are interstate listings, national listings, vignettes describing waiting children in adoption newsletters, and foreign listings. Social workers looking for parents talk to social workers looking for children. Everyone is looking for a match.

Sometimes this all feels like shopping for a mail-order child, but it is a necessary process because the possibilities become more concrete. Prospective parents refine their desires and confront their own limitations as they look at the pictures and read the write-ups on the children available for adoption.

- What does the information in the listing really mean?
- Do I want a handicapped child?
- What handicaps can I deal with?
- What about a child with learning disabilities?
- What support will I get if I adopt a child of another race?
- Could I handle a sibling group? How many would I consider?
- What can my extended family accept? I want my child to have aunts, uncles, and grandparents. What if they cannot accept my child?
- What is the oldest child I could adopt?
- What would it be like parenting a child who has been abused?

In a typical adoption prospective parents eventually find two or three children in the listings that they think they would like to parent. They ask their social worker to see if one of them is still available. Their home study is given to the child's social worker, who decides from all the home studies he or she receives which parents to consider. Parents who are being seriously considered for a particular child are given more information about the child's history, behavior, and possible problems. Eventually, if the decision is made to place, the parents and children meet; this is an exciting time.

❧ When we went to meet the kids and spend the night with them in the hotel, we were really nervous. As we drove across town, "Let's Spend the Night Together" played on the radio. We were hysterical. I liked it a lot.

Jose was thirteen, kind of chubby, with curly hair. He was trying to swagger, but he was still too small. Rosa, eleven, had her hair combed straight back the way they made her do it in the orphanage. She looked beautiful, but she has never combed it like that since. David, at ten, was so small I could hold him in my lap. By the end of the visit Elizabeth and I had decided that we wanted to do this, but the social worker made us go home to think it over. The kids were really mad when we got on the plane and they didn't. I remember my wife crying. She wanted her kids to be with her. We were pretty attached.

A week later they came. We picked them up at the airport and drove them home. We went to the shore for a week and had a nice time. Everyone was on good behavior. When we got back, they started school, and things began to get interesting.

Egan Packard, about Jose, Rosa, and David, thirteen, eleven, and ten when placed, twenty, eighteen, and seventeen now.

Even when everything everybody knows is openly shared, there is a lot unknown about an older child who is available for adoption. Records are incomplete, and few children have the same social worker throughout placement. Children who don't feel safe don't talk about what happened to them and how they feel about it. Many were abandoned or abused when they were pre-verbal, so they can't make sense of their feelings. They just stuff them. Stuffed feelings erupt at various developmental stages. This makes older child adoption very risky. Social workers owe it to prospective adoptive parents to be open with them, to let them read the complete records, to talk to foster parents, school personnel, and therapists. Even then, what they know will only be the tip of the iceberg.

If anything parents hear makes them decide not to adopt a particular child, they weren't meant to be that child's parents. If they are discouraged by hearing about the condition the child is in and cannot focus on the strengths the child has, they could never live with that child. The honest social worker will have saved the parents from adopting the wrong child, and the child from another damaging move. What discourages one parent might not discourage another. There will be people who are not blind to the condition the child is in, who may even be discouraged by it, but who, after talking with other families and finding out about services, decide to proceed. Covering up is not the answer. Calvin's social worker was as honest as they come, and yet Milton Yardley decided to proceed.

❧ If I had been asked to paint a cover for *Tom Sawyer* or *Huckleberry Finn*, I couldn't have had a better model than Calvin. His face showed impudence, audacity, and was nice looking. He was presented to me as a youngster who had been hurt by his biological family and abused in two foster homes. The social worker said, "The best you can expect from this youngster is an obnoxious house guest for the next eight to ten years."

"Is there not one good thing you could say about this boy?" I asked.

"I was going to adopt him myself, but my wife said no, because we had just adopted one like him. He has the potential to be a strong, decent, intelligent human being, but you may never see it. I offer you no hope, but it's there. I'm not going to introduce you to this kid unless you are prepared beforehand to make a complete and total commitment. There is no stunt that we can pull off that will keep Calvin from knowing he is on the block, and he can't deal with that anymore. Go home and think about it, talk to your support system, and call me after seventy-two hours."

I talked to my parents, who thought I was crazy, but they said, "Go ahead, if this is what you want to do." I believed everything the social worker said, but I knew love conquers all. I knew that I was a strong, stable person who had every intention of standing by this boy no matter what. I had worked with scouts, taught for twenty-five years, had success with youngsters with whom other people had had difficulties. My track record was good. I assumed this was the winning combination, that there was nothing a thirteen-year-old boy could do over the next five years that I couldn't keep one step ahead of. How wrong I was!

In a couple of weeks I was standing in a large sunny kitchen looking over a yard full of children playing in the snow. One kid picked up a huge block of ice and brought it crashing down on another kid's head. "Calvin?" I asked. "Calvin," the worker said. From November to February we exchanged visits every weekend. He seemed to have dealt with the demons of his past, or was willing to deal with them, and it felt like a very nice match. In February he moved in. For two summers and into the autumn of the second year he was everything anyone ever wanted from a son.

The one thing I did not do and absolutely should have done was to get Calvin tested and into counseling. My social worker told me that, but I didn't see the point. No symptoms appeared except immaturity. I planned to do it when I needed to, but by then it was too late. In the autumn of his freshman year of high school, Calvin changed.

One night he called me at work, "Dad, I want to have a sleepover."

"You haven't been to school all week. We're not going to do that. You may have a sleepover when you have been in school the five days before."

He called me three more times, each time more angry and less willing to accept my decision.

Finally he said, "If you don't come home, you're going to be sorry. I'm going to have a sleepover."

I responded, "Calvin, two things. Number one, I don't respond to ultimatums. Number two, you're not going to have a sleepover."

I finished my work and went home.

I couldn't open the door when I got there. Everything in the house was smashed. He was asleep, or shamming sleep, with his thumb in his mouth. I looked at him, thought some wild thoughts, turned around, drove the car to a night-owl store and bought a pack of gum. I don't chew gum. I sat in the car and chewed five sticks, one after another, until the flavor was gone while I thought through what I was going to do. Then I drove home, woke Calvin up, and said, "We've got some cleaning up to do, then we've got some serious talking to do."

He burst into tears and we cleaned the place up.

I told him, "There was a lot of damage done, and it's got to be paid for. The things that are broken are things we don't have any more, and we won't have them until you can pay for them. We can rebuild our home, and we can rebuild our lives, but you're going to get some counseling."

After that things became easier to deal with.

Milton Yardley, single parent of Calvin, thirteen when placed, twenty-one now.

When the stuffed feelings of an angry toddler erupt in an adolescent, it can be dangerous. Therapy can relieve the pressure of unresolved issues. The earlier this happens, the better.

As heartbreaking as life became for Calvin's single dad when Calvin changed, his dad didn't have to deal with feelings that the social worker had betrayed him. He felt he was treated fairly and honestly, had gone into the adoption knowing what there was to be known. The rest was a risk he had been willing to take.

Giving birth to a child is a risk. Adopting a baby is a greater risk because the child's genetic heritage and quality of prenatal care is unknown. Adopting an older child is a still greater risk because, in addition, the emotional residue of the life the child has lived until the time of the adoption creates a potential time bomb. The idealism and naiveté of most adoptive parents discount the risks. Like most expectant parents, they focus on the newness of life and the possibilities ahead with great hope and excitement.

A Family that Feels Different

Parents who have been with a child from the beginning know what has gone before. Parents of an older adopted child often find themselves unexpectedly looking through a window into the child's past and having to deal with the feelings that this evokes. Their children were not always theirs.

❧ I would like to live in a perfect world, but I know that's not possible. I have a good friend from Zaire who shows me things that make me sick, so I know the world is not perfect. I did not realize to what extent I had tried to live in my perfect world until I adopted Millie. None of us is perfect, but we are all "God drops." Everything good in us is of God, and we are called to bring that goodness to our corner of the world.

I could see the goodness in Millie but she couldn't, and it hurt me that this little girl couldn't see that she was a God drop. That's what hurts me in all the abused children of the world. Their God drop has been pushed in the corner so they don't see it. My work with Millie is to help her see her God drop and let the painful memories and hurt go as best she can. I hold her when she sobs, and unless she wants to share her hurt I never probe. We talk afterward, but I know from my birth children that memories are both less and more than what really happened, so I listen to the pain, not the circumstances.

It's like being with someone who has lost a loved one. Millie has lost her childhood. The other day I was sitting in a sandbox with a two year old. We had Frisbees and I said, "You make a lemon pie and I'll make a strawberry one." We giggled, took our shoes off, and wiggled our toes in the sand. Millie just watched, and I could see the pain in her: That didn't happen to me. I wasn't considered a gift until I came to this house.

Angela Jackson, about Millie, ten when placed, twelve now.

Some feelings are not so private and touching. Children can make a family into a spectacle, and that's never easy to handle.

🌿 Nobody ever told me that I would be embarrassed in public at every opportunity. If I took Barry to the supermarket with me, when we'd get to the check-out line he'd say, "Are you going to lock me in the closet this afternoon?" and I'd get "You awful parent" looks.

If I went with his brother, Jared—Mr. Gregarious Charm—he carried on conversations like, "My what a lovely store you have, Ma'am," and people would say, "What a wonderful child you have, it must be in the genes." We couldn't go anywhere unnoticed. For a long time they were "My children whom I adopted" because their behavior was so unacceptable to me that I felt I had to explain them.

After we'd had them two or three years we registered Barry in summer camp but didn't tell them he was adopted because he was doing better. If Barry acted out, the teachers put him in the time-out chair for five minutes. He'd ask, "Are you going to beat me now?" They began to wonder if they should report us for child abuse. One day Barry wore his "Superman Was Adopted Too" T-shirt, so the teachers asked, "Barry, are you adopted?"

"No."

When my mother went to pick him up that day, they asked her, and she explained the situation to them.

Craig and Mitzi Clark, about Barry and Jared, three and four when placed, eleven and twelve now.

Parenting older adopted children usually starts with a brief "honeymoon" period; after that it is more a commitment than a relationship for a very long time. These children are very afraid of closeness, so it takes them a long time to reciprocate honestly, or at all. At best, it feels like loving someone who doesn't love you. At worse, it feels like loving someone who finds your love unacceptable.

🌿 My last adoption was a sibling group of three whose international adoption was disrupting. I got the call just before Christmas five years ago. "If you don't take them, we'll have to send the older two back to El Salvador and find a home for the younger one."

How do you say "there's no room in the inn" just before Christmas?

I was told, "There is nothing wrong with the kids. The family they went to expected too much."

Hell would be a good description of the early years with these sweet, adorable children. When Rafael is mad at me, he'll pee in the middle of the bathroom floor and put a mat over it so the next person will squish in. "I missed the toilet," he says. Sure.

Nina, the oldest, was fourteen when she came. She had been through three orphanages when her mother died. When people die they become saints and El Salvador became the land of milk and honey. Isobel, the youngest, was the first to learn English. She wanted to belong, but Nina held her back.

Older child adoptions are hard. There are days when I wonder what I've gotten myself into. Who do I think I am that I can do this when others have failed? Will I have to pay with my whole family? I adopted four children at birth, and they had to put up with a lot because of my decision to adopt older children.

I've reached the point where I ask myself: Why did I do this? I could be living in a nice condo, going to the theater every week. Did I need this? I must have. I've come to think that success is not how the kids turn out but doing my best day after day. I like being a mother, and I enjoy my kids in lots of ways. Nina has such a lovely smile, and seeing her use it now is almost worth everything. I don't ask for big rewards.

May Udall, single parent of Nina, Rafael, and Isobel, four-teen, twelve and eight when placed, nineteen, seventeen, and thirteen now.

All feelings, not just the nice ones, need to be acknowledged, otherwise the tyranny of the "ought" or "ought not" makes the situation unendurable. Honesty is a survival skill for parenting difficult children because recognizing and admitting how you feel is like taking the lid off the kettle to let the steam out. In a pressured family situation, letting the steam off in a supportive environment has to happen regularly for health and abuse prevention.

❧ My husband called from work one day. "How's it going?"

"I'm the best mother in the whole world because Jose took me to the edge—I wanted to kill him with my bare hands—and I didn't."

"You know, you're right."

The kids make it so personal. Jose's not mad at me. He's mad at the world, and he hates himself. He doesn't know what he'd like to do to his birth mom, so he's taking it out on me.

The big theories are nature versus nurture, and we've got neither going for us. They're not our kids biologically, and there's this huge amount of time when we didn't nurture them, so we didn't bring them up. Even so, I sit and think, What did I do wrong? Then I remember a friend who once said to his daughter, "You had a terrible adolescence. I went through it with you, but I didn't give it to you."

Elizabeth Packard, about Jose, thirteen when placed, twenty now.

A Family that Looks Different

Adoptive families often look more like the human family than a typical American family. In some, the children come in various shades, several languages, multiple ethnic backgrounds. Bonding needs to transcend diversity, and this adds to the challenge. So does the need to deal with the public's inability to be comfortable with diversity.

🌶 Our family has two white birth children and two who were foster children; Cathy is Hispanic and Ann is black. When we first started going out as a family, two white kids, one brown, and one black, people stared at us. I wanted to say, "Bug off!" I don't care anymore. We're a nice family, our differences are obvious, and people are dealing with it. That's their thing.

Cathy came to us in foster care when she was ten months old. Her birth mother visited until Cathy was two and a half. She was frightened of her birth mother, who used to do mean things like give her a bottle and then take it away while she was still drinking. One time she trapped Cathy in the playhouse and wouldn't let her out. I had to rescue her. After the visits Cathy would wake up in the middle of the night with dreams. Caseworkers kept changing.

The birth mother wouldn't see Cathy for months, and then she would start the case up again. I understand that parents have to have every opportunity to get themselves together before their rights are terminated, but it's difficult to watch when you really care about their kid.

When her parents' rights were finally terminated, we were told we couldn't adopt Cathy because we're white and she's Hispanic. After waiting two more years, the decision was reversed. We received Cathy at ten months and couldn't officially adopt her until she was seven years old.

Ann was four when she came as a foster child. We were just giving her mother a break. After several months I ran into Ann's mother in the grocery store, and she asked me if we'd adopt Ann.

"We can't adopt her. She's black, we're white. Social Services would never let us do it!"

"I can't mother her, I can't nurture her, I want her to stay with you."

Social Services thought Ann needed a black family, and we didn't know what we wanted. We just wanted what was best for Ann. Everybody was hitting us with all the negatives: when she becomes an adolescent she's going to rebel against you; she's going to be angry that she was raised by whites; she's going to wish she was raised by blacks; she's going to wish she were white. We could have problems with our birth kids too, I thought, but I'm not going to lose Ann because I'm afraid of what's going to happen in a few years. So we talked to Ann and the rest of the family. We decided to adopt her.

I'm always concerned about our having black friends. We were friends with one black family, but they moved. I see black families at basketball games, and one of these days I'm going to walk up to one of them and say, "Black family, will you be our friend?" I've tried to get a big sister for Ann, but it just hasn't worked out.

The legal work for Ann's adoption was completed a few months before Cathy's, but we waited and their adoptions were finalized together. I could not go through Ann's while Cathy waited, when she had been with us five years longer. We got permission to have the ceremony in the court room and invited all our friends. When the judge had finished he said, "I have never had an adoption so well attended." We had a big party afterward. We wanted those two girls to know how special they are to us. I was so happy to have it over with. With the adoption announcement we sent out the following poem:

> We come in many shades and sizes, many colors too.
> Our languages are many, our cultures quite a few.
> But for all our variations there's one thing we all
>   share,
> We're molded in His image and protected in His
>   care.
> A father to all children, His arms are open wide,
> To welcome every one of us, He's always at our side.
> And when our troubles daunt us, on His loving
>   grace we call,
> For whatever race, color, or creed, Our Lord loves us
>   all.

Katrina Adkins, about Cathy and Ann, ten months and four years when placed, both eight now.

More attention needs to be given to the issue of background when a child is first placed so that these Solomon-like decisions don't have to occur so often. Two principles are in conflict here: the need for a child to have consistent parenting for attachment purposes, and the need for a child to have parents of the same ethnic background for identity formation. But how do you think Cathy would have felt had she been removed from her mother of six years in order to be adopted by a stranger who happened to be Hispanic? There is evidence that multiple moves damage children more than being part of a transracial family does. The same issue delayed Ann's adoption.

The important thing is that children have help finding out who they are and that they don't feel like foreigners in their own family. In a birth family children get their ethnic identity from their parents. In an adoptive family everyone adds his or her difference to the whole.

❧ When Rhoda, Richard, and Rickie were younger I made Korean food and had Korean flags on the wall. They had a box of Korean things that they used for show and tell at school. But all that did was tell them they were different when the important thing was to be part of the family. So we celebrated their birthdays, the day they came to the family, and told them that if they ever want to go to

Korea we would take them. Rhoda chose to go to China with her high school class instead. Richard was afraid to go because he was told they might prevent his leaving and induct him into the military. Rickie wasn't interested in going.

Shirley Newman, about Rhoda, Rickie, and Richard, two, eleven, and five when placed separately, twenty-two, twenty-five, and twenty-three now.

During children's middle years it is important for them to feel part of a family, to know how they fit in. Differences can be acknowledged but not emphasized. During adolescence the opposite is the case.

❧   The kids think it's funny when people say, "How come your name's Packard?" to them or when they meet me. I'm 6'2" and pale, while they're shorter and dark. David is actually growing. He's 5'6" and I'm convinced it's because he wants to look like me. They are all trying to find out what it means to be who they are. Puerto Rico for Jose means platanos, empanadas, and the Bronx. Rosa started out thinking it was a way of talking or walking; now she's figured out it's a history and a culture. She says, "I don't know why they call us minorities; there's nothing wrong with us." David is much more interested in who he is than in his ethnic background.

Egan Packard, about Jose, Rosa, and David, thirteen, eleven, and ten when placed, twenty, eighteen, and seventeen now.

A Family that Needs a Different Extended Family

Adoptive parents cannot change the color of their skin or their ethnic make up, but they can explore their children's cultural heritage with them and create an intentional extended family that reflects the racial and ethnic diversity in their nuclear adoptive family. For parents and children it is helpful also to include other adoptive families in their extended family. Of course this is not meant to exclude the parents' blood relatives. It is simply helpful, and sometimes necessary, to supplement what they can bring to the situation in understanding and support.

The Abbot family created an extended family by keeping contact with the Hispanic birth relatives of several of their children. The Adkins family sought compatible families in their neighborhood whose ethnic background is similar to their children's. Such families can provide role models for children and an entry to an intercultural social life for the parents.

Adoption groups exist in many cities and can be accessed through the agency through which the adoption took place, Adoptive Families of America, or even in the Yellow Pages. In adoption groups children don't feel different because they are adopted, and they can talk with peers about their experience. Parents can blow off steam in a way that people who haven't adopted older children might misunderstand.

❧ My original family is very nice when we visit, but neither my brother nor sister would take the kids if something happened to me. They wouldn't know what to do with them.

When Dolores came, I realized that I needed a different kind of extended family. So I started inviting families from our church and adoption support group over for supper. With adoptive families I could feel comfortable "letting it all out." I learned what other people were dealing with, and how. When Dolores did something I didn't understand, or I needed an opinion on how to deal with a situation, I knew who to call. I'm hotheaded, and I need a sounding board who's not so emotionally involved. It was a challenge every day to get the behavior that was necessary in a situation without getting into a control battle. Instead of playing the Lone Ranger I learned to reach out for help when everything got too big for me. My parenting years were the most alive I've had, but I would have been overwhelmed rather than energized if I hadn't had such a supportive extended family.

Hope Walker, single mother of three children adopted separately.

Some extended birth families do the best they can, but they don't consider being adopted equal to being born into the family, and the day comes when they let their attitude out. Parents adopting a child cannot assume that their parents and siblings have adopted the child in their hearts. There can be unexpected announcements, like those in the next two vignettes.

❧ My parents and siblings hugged my girls, but I didn't think they felt the same about the girls we adopted as about the boys who

were born to us. One year my mother had a set of diamond earrings she was going to give away because my dad had given her a
new set for their anniversary. We were kidding around the kitchen
table about it.

"Who's going to get these earrings?"

"Whoever gets them should have girls to hand them down to."

"That leaves just me and Karen," I said.

"Mainly me," replied Karen. My children are blood to Grandma."

It bothers me that I can't make them accept my children fully,
but I don't dwell on it. I'm just glad we don't live near them, so
we don't have contact all that often.

*Katrina Adkins, about Cathy and Ann, ten months and four
years old when placed, both eight now.*

● Six years ago my parents showed me their fiftieth wedding announcement in the newspaper. It said they were the parents of two
daughters and the grandparents of nine. I said, "Nine grandchildren! Did you tell them this is a mistake?" I have seven birth children and my sister has two. Then I realized that they had never
counted the adopted children.

"Mom, you never counted Richard, Rhoda, and Rickie? Dad,
your mother was adopted!"

"Her parents were married. They died in an accident."

They had sent the children birthday and Christmas presents,
and never made their feelings known. It was really hard for me to
believe that they had never accepted the children, because I had, of
course.

That summer my parents were coming to visit.

"We're adopting a little boy from Chicago."

"Is he American?"

"Yes."

When they arrived they said, "We didn't know you had adopted
a colored child."

"They're called black."

"You told us he was American."

"He is."

They left three days later saying they would never come to our
house again. When we adopted two more children my mother said,

"What have we ever done to make you treat us this way?" I knew more than I acknowledged to myself that this would be their reaction, but it didn't stop me. It's so sad.

Shirley Newman. The Newmans have birth children and children adopted when they were older from North America, South America, Europe, and Asia.

Some grandparents accept the children when all goes well but aren't supportive when the going gets rough.

🐾 Before Calvin and my mother met, my mother said, "He's thirteen years old, and I'm not going to embarrass him by hugging him. I'm not going to cry." When we got to their house Calvin leaped out of the car and went running to her with his arms out, and she burst into tears and hugged him. They were sure I had done the right thing. I had taken this boy from a wretched situation, I was saving him from harm's way, and he was a respectful grandchild. He was the apple of their eye until he trashed my house.

Then they were hurt, stunned, could find no explanation. They wanted me to pack him up and send him back. I kept saying, "Mom and Dad, you can't ask me to do that. You are asking me to do something you wouldn't do yourselves. What I know about love and loyalty I learned from you. You would not have abandoned me, no matter what I had done."

There was a period of time when I couldn't even call them. My friends at work did not really understand what I was going through, and I knew no other single adoptive parents.

Milton Yardley, single parent of Calvin, thirteen when placed, twenty-one now.

It's one thing for families to support family members in adopting and another to be committed fully to the unconditional love of the children or even the unconditional support of their parents. Because this parent had no support group, he was very alone as he continued to parent his son. Actually, what helped him the most was adopting a second son, Daniel.

🐾 When I adopted Daniel I could see that even though I was raising him under stress, I was getting normal reactions. I could see through

Daniel that I wasn't a bad parent, I was just the father of a really tough kid and one who's growing up right. I have my feet of clay, but I can still stand on both of them.

Milton Yardley, single parent of Daniel, thirteen when placed, nineteen now.

Having a child other than the one causing the difficulties at the moment is not only affirming but can provide balance in a situation.

❧ Sometimes I've felt that I'm in quicksand and everything is lost if I don't have something to hold onto. When I was losing Dolores, Clara came, so Dolores could take herself away, but she couldn't deprive me of having a family. When I was losing Clara, I had Curt to hold onto. When I began losing him, I started building a life for myself. Whatever he does, I will still have me.

Hope Walker, single parent of three children adopted separately.

Couples who can be truly honest with each other give each other great support.

❧ My wife and I go out on a date once a week come hell or high water, and we're really honest with each other. Some days I tell her I can't stand to look at Andy one more minute because of his behavior. Even though we believe that what he's doing is not a personal attack on us, it *feels* personal and gets overwhelming. But we walk in forgiveness. There isn't a day that goes by without our hugging him and telling him that we love him. We've made that commitment. But we have also agreed that we are not going to rip the rest of our family apart over him.

Gail and Hector Garrett, about Andy, seven when placed, thirteen now.

Individuals can find support in the situation, couples in each other, but an extended family is also important—an adopted extended family in addition to the blood relatives of the adoptive parents, who may or may not be able to be supportive. Parents need to provide not only for their children but also for themselves, particularly when there is little reciprocity in their relationship with their children.

8

A Family that Needs Services

Apart from living with the older adopted child, the greatest challenge for an adoptive parent is determining the child's need and then obtaining appropriate services from the educational, social-services, and mental-health systems. Many children have multiple special needs. Emotional issues can trigger behavioral problems and learning disabilities. Medical and physical problems can overshadow other issues. It can be difficult to determine which issue might be causing a particular problem, or whether several are "colliding and colluding." Knowing which issue is related to which need or behavior is important, because it can affect how to address the situation.

❧ Tam has a physical handicap, and most people focus on that because it is obvious. But he also has some learning problems that were overlooked. Professionals made assumptions without looking at his record or consulting with us. When Tam was in fourth grade, we became aware that he was having some reading problems. We asked his teacher what help he was getting and discovered that even though she knew he was having trouble she hadn't referred him for extra help because, "You can't expect him to read when he is still learning English." She had assumed he was a recent Asian adoptee. We pointed out that he had been speaking English since nursery school and had a pretty good grasp of the language. He got help.

Natalie and Brady O'Malley, about Tam, three when placed, twenty-five now.

Parents of most children are very aware of their needs and invested in their success. Parents cannot assume the same acuity in professionals who are dealing with classrooms or caseloads of children. Professionals, in turn, need to look upon parents as the experts regarding their child. This expertise places the parents on a par with the educational and mental-health professionals at the conference tables around which decisions are made about what services the child will receive. It is easy for the professionals to think that they know it all and for the parents to fall into the supplicant role. When this happens, the child receives the services the system is prepared to provide. They may or may not be what the child needs.

Securing Appropriate Educational Services

When a school-aged child comes to live in pre-adoptive placement, the first step for adoptive parents is to bring any existing school records to the local school and register the child. During the first year of placement the focus for the child's adjustment has to be at home, and if the child can maintain himself or herself at school, he or she is to be congratulated. Therefore it is important that the school placement be at or below the level the child is coming from. If the child has been given a special-education classification, adoptive parents need to know that and have the documentation. Sometimes the local school system will accept that classification. Sometimes the school district will insist on its own testing and evaluation before it will decide on a placement, particularly if the previous records show that testing has not been done for the child for over two years.

❧   By the time we got Raymond we had established a relationship with the school district. Raymond had been classified with good documentation in the school district of his first pre-adoptive placement, so his classification in our district was fairly routine. He was placed in an appropriate program within a month and maintained acceptable behavior there for a year and a half.

     Then Raymond began acting out and the principal started sending him home for various reasons—suspending him without suspending him. I insisted that he document the suspensions, which meant that he had to go before the school board to prove need. If a child is classified as having emotional problems, suspending him on the basis of his disability is illegal.

The Committee on Special Education (CSE) was called to review Raymond's placement. The principal wanted to put Raymond on home tutoring. We wanted to look into the possibility of medication and other therapeutic supports. The CSE delayed implementation until these avenues could be explored, and eventually we agreed on a special-education class in a special school located outside the district. He has been doing well there for two years and now we are looking at the possibility of his moving into a less restrictive environment within the district.

Craig and Mitzi Clark, about Raymond, six when placed, ten now.

If parents agree with their child's previous testing and placement decisions but their school district refuses to accept the classification with which their child comes, parents can challenge the district's decision. Children going through the strain of adjusting to a new family and a new school don't need to be set up to fail by having their past educational difficulties ignored.

❧ Dolores came classified learning disabled (LD). I took her documentation to the local elementary school to enroll her in the system, and I was told she should attend the regular classroom until a meeting could be held to decide on her placement. This made no sense to me, so I said I would keep her home until then. I was asked to bring her to an interview with the school psychologist. The interview began during a class period. Dolores was so attentive and appropriate that I began to question the classification. The bell rang for the change of classes and Dolores was transformed. Not a part of her was quiet. Her feet danced. She looked almost spastic. The interview ended with the psychologist asking me to keep her home until a space in an appropriate classroom could be found.

Hope Walker, about Dolores, twelve when placed, nineteen now.

All children, including the mentally, emotionally, and physically handicapped, have the right to an appropriate education at public expense. Adoptive parents must act as guardians of that right for their children. When a family sees that a child's educational needs are not being met in the classroom where he or she is placed, the parents can make a written request for a hearing. The CSE must convene a meeting, and an Individualized Education Program (IEP) must be developed to meet those needs. Of course this IEP may not be in agreement with the parents' view of their child's needs and how these should be met.

Prolonged suspension or expulsion is one indication that a child's needs are not being met. In Raymond's case, the parents' requiring written documentation concerning the suspensions held the school system accountable and resulted in a more appropriate placement for their child.

According to their needs at a given time, children can move along the continuum of more restrictive or less restrictive environments.

LEAST RESTRICTIVE

Regular class

Regular class with in-class accommodations

Regular class with supplemental services

Part-time special-education class in regular school

Full-time special-education class in regular school

Special education in a special school

Home instruction

Residential school

Hospital School

MOST RESTRICTIVE

Not all options are available in the neighborhood school or even in the school district, so some placements may require bussing. As the placement becomes more restrictive, it becomes more expensive. Parents who don't know their rights can end up with the bill.

🖙 My daughter Clara was placed by the court in a residential school out of district because she could not live at home. She had been maintaining herself in a regular classroom in a regular school. The head of special education in my district told me, "We don't have to pay for her education there because we can provide for her here. She has been sent there because she cannot live at home." I believed him and paid for her last two years of school. I have since read school law, and it is my understanding that in such cases the school system where the parent resides is required to pay the educational but not the residential expenses. In this case my ignorance cost me a considerable amount of money. I thought that I would be given what I had a right to. I learned that I have to know my rights and fight for them.

In the case of my son Curtis, he had not been classified but was scheduled for testing because his teacher had requested it. So I asked my school system to go from there. The school asked me to keep him home until the process was complete. Having learned my rights, I requested that he have a home-bound teacher while we waited.

Because Curtis had just had two disrupted adoptive placements, he was fragile. His therapist, hoping to avoid hospitalization, requested that he be placed directly into a day-treatment program. The school system refused. He was placed in a school for emotionally disturbed learning disabled (EDLD) children. After a month Curtis started refusing to use his seat belt on the bus, putting nooses on trees, and talking about hanging himself. He was hospitalized for several months, after which he was placed in the day-treatment program his therapist had originally requested for him. I was frustrated that he hadn't been placed there when we requested it. It meant his having to deal with more changes. When I counted them up, Curtis had had three families and seven schools in one year!

Hope Walker, single parent of Clara, thirteen when placed, eighteen now, and Curtis, nine when placed, twelve now.

When school or treatment placement can be expedited by listening to parents and professionals who know the child well, it should be. More often children are left to prove by their behavior over and over again that they need a more restrictive environment. They have to fail. This process is painful to watch, harmful to the child's self-image, and wastes time.

Older child adoption provides a challenge to the school system because it brings into its census children with problems it hasn't had to deal with before and parents articulate about the children's needs and the school system's responsibilities. School-system personnel seek to offer adequate services at minimum cost, while the parents want the best for their children. Each side has a different bottom line, and this heightens the tension of the debate.

❧ Derek and Theo are both in English as a second language (ESL). Theo started school in first grade. At the first conference one teacher talked about how little progress he had made, and the other said, "He doesn't belong in first grade." We agreed he needed special education. I visited that department and requested that Theo be tested for learning disabilities.

"We can't test him because his English isn't good enough and he has cerebral palsy."

"You can't test him?"

"Not for three or four years."

"You mean Theo is going to sit in a classroom without any special help except ESL for three or four years?"

"That's correct."

I bit my lip, didn't say another word, went home, and called the State Department of Education. It took me three days to find the right person. Her response was,"Are you sure they said that?"

"Ask them."

I documented everything in writing. Theo was tested as much as he could be and at the next meeting the director of special education still refused to allow Theo in the special-ed room.

"You'd rather see Theo in the hall with his aide than in the special-ed room where he belongs?"

It took a while, but now Theo has ESL in the morning and is in the special-ed room in the afternoon. He also has speech and occupational therapy.

It was hard. Because I bucked the school the teachers looked the other way when I came in. I commented to the principal, "I don't understand some of the teachers here. They go into education because they love children, and yet when a parent speaks up for her child, the parent becomes the enemy."

At one point the special-education director came to the house. I introduced her to the three youngest, whom she didn't know about yet: "Robin is a cocaine baby, Paul probably is, and Teresa's been burned over 37 percent of her body."

"We don't have such children in our school!"

"Well, now you know mine are coming, so you have to be ready for them."

Shirley Newman, about five of her children.

If school personnel do not have much experience with certain special needs, they may make decisions based on opinions and assumptions rather than facts. In these cases parents, with more information, expertise, and accurate data, are critical as advocates for their child.

Some parents find and pay for an alternative if they perceive that what the school system is providing is not adequate. They take the responsibility for getting the child capable of benefiting from a regular classroom rather than requiring the school system to meet his or her needs. They play catch-up outside the system so as to fit into it. The child meets the school's expectations rather than the school meeting the child's needs.

✍ Dennis went to the local elementary school through sixth grade. He couldn't read words with more than three letters, and even that was guesswork. I went to a teacher's meeting and was told, "Dennis is doing wonderfully." I thought, he's not doing wonderfully, he's not learning anything at all. My boy is in sixth grade and he can't read a menu! I decided to get him out of that school, so I went from one school to another in town and ended up at a small religious school. The teacher said, "Maybe we could take Dennis next year."

"I'll get down on my knees and beg you. Take Dennis right now."

"Well, all right!"

It cost $150 a month, which really hurt us. I had to take him in the morning and pick him up at night, which was a nuisance, but within six months he could read. Every night he came home, did his homework, and was proud of it. When Dennis finished eighth grade the teacher said, "I think he's ready for regular school," and he was.
Darlene Olson, about Dennis, seven when placed, sixteen now.

Sometimes the story doesn't end that way. There can be a lot of improvement, but the child still needs services, as was the case with Jody.

✍ I chose to home-school Jody in seventh grade because the school said it couldn't give him the services he needed, and I wasn't willing to put him through making them do it. They only saw his behavioral and emotional problems, and I was sure he had a learning disability in math. I had him tested, and I was right. I worked with him at home the way they had told me to work with the disability. Even though he was very noncompliant about doing school work, I managed to catch him up to grade level in everything.

By the middle of eighth grade Jody had worn me down, so I asked the school to home-teach him the last quarter and get him an LD teacher for math. I knew my rights. I wrote letters and made phone calls trying to get the school system to offer special services. I sent the documentation three times, but nobody had it. Finally I got up one morning, dressed professionally, put the documentation in my briefcase, went to the school, and said, "This is a special-services child, and this is what needs to be done. I can be nice about it or not." The school decided to comply. By the end of the day he was scheduled for special services. We shouldn't have to fight for these kids, but we do.

It's hard to make a case for emotional and learning disabilities. We had less trouble negotiating with the school for our daughter Sophie because her problems are physical, not behavioral. She's brain-damaged and has to be patterned to learn. It takes her longer to do things. "I'll get it done," she says. Then she smiles, and you want her to be normal.

Karen Kane, about Jody, eight when placed, seventeen now, and Sophie, three when placed, ten now.

Jody's mom didn't want to put him through what it would take to require the school system to provide services. She had a choice, because she was an at-home mom. Heather's mom had to work full-time. Because she was a special-education teacher by profession, she knew the law and could advocate effectively, but it wasn't easy.

💰 When Heather was coming to live with me in pre-adoptive placement, I went to the school she had been attending, got copies of her records, and encouraged them to change her grade level. She didn't know the sounds of any letters of the alphabet, so to say she was a fourth grader was ridiculous. Since Heather had psychosocial dwarfism, she didn't look like a fourth grader either.

Heather started at her new school in an interim placement for the multiply handicapped on May 1. Soon after that we had our first meeting to develop an Individual Education Plan (IEP) for Heather. I am a special-education professional, but I went to the meeting as a parent and felt overwhelmed by the committee. I was amazed. Halfway through the meeting I realized what was happening, and that in reality I knew more about Heather than anyone else at the table. So I asked, "What do you know about psychosocial dwarfism?" They knew nothing, so I summarized the literature on the subject. They agreed to leave Heather in the class for the multiply handicapped but refused to give her speech.

"My daughter needs speech."

"You can't tell us that."

"Don't tell me I can't tell you that. Listen to her talk. Speech has been on her IEP since she started school." She got speech, and everything went well until Heather heard that her foster sister in the home she had come from had been adopted by the foster parents who had not adopted Heather.

Heather regressed to crawling on the floor and refusing to do anything. I went to the school, informed them of what had happened and that we were working on the situation in therapy. A week later I received a letter stating that the school wanted to have a meeting to decide on a change of placement for Heather. I told the school that I would not agree to a move for Heather at this time because she was already suffering from rejection, she loves her teacher, and she would experience being moved to another classroom as another rejection. I would have requested an impartial hearing at that point, and they knew it, so they agreed not to move her. I agreed to their putting counseling on the IEP, provided the school counselor dealt only with school issues. She has private counseling for the adoption issues.

When they scheduled the annual review, I wrote asking them to change the date because I had to be out of the country. The teacher said, "You don't really need to come, there are no changes." But I wanted to be there. The meeting was held anyway, and the school system requested a change of placement. The classroom teacher left the room, refusing to continue the meeting in my absence.

When the meeting was reconvened, they wanted to change Heather's classification from multiply handicapped because she had no physical handicap. I countered, "She is not orthopedically impaired, but psycho-social dwarfism is a physical handicap. Because she grows when she is sleeping, Heather requires twelve hours sleep a night, plus a nap in the afternoon. This affects her academically."

"Let's go to the law."

"Fine."

We took out a copy of the law and read the definition of physically handicapped.

"According to our interpretation, Heather does not qualify."

"I was a member of the team that did the training of administrators and staff on the interpretation of the law. I know Heather qualifies."

Her classification remained multiply handicapped, and she worked in the same classroom for another year. It was good for her because the teacher was strong, and it put Heather in a position to help other kids.

By the following year I knew Heather was ready for a change. I informed the school system that I was ready for Heather to have a new program and asked what they had to offer. They decided they needed a psychiatric evaluation. It was supposed to be done during the summer, but it wasn't, so in September Heather returned to the same classroom. Immediately the special-education director called for a review, and I asked, "What are you going to review? A psychiatric has not been done."

They scheduled it with the doctor who had seen Heather when she first came. The psychiatrist asked us to stand. We did.

"She's not a dwarf."

"I know her," Heather said. "The assistant principal brought her out to the playground to meet me."

This was supposed to be an impartial evaluation.

The psychiatrist spent fifteen minutes with Heather, then put her at a table to color and called me in.

"She manipulates you, and you spoil her."

"I don't spoil her. I'm very strict with her. Are we here to judge my parenting skills or Heather's emotional state?"

"Heather says you like to take naps too."

"When I can afford the luxury, yes. You must see a big change in her."

"She still presents the same way."

"Do you mean as an emotionally disturbed, developmentally delayed child?"

"What private schools have you gone to see? What is your agenda?"

"I don't know what's appropriate for her."

"I think we have a school in our system for her. She needs a new medical."

"That will be done by her private doctor." The psychiatrist had her secretary take Heather's height and weight.

"The medical won't be necessary."

"What do you mean by 'She presents the same way?'"

"Retarded."

Heather is not retarded. I called the child advocate to help me deal with due process. She came to all the meetings with me, which put the school system on alert, and gave me support. In addition, she documented everything that was said. We got our own psychiatric and a psycho-neurological examination. We picked doctors who were renowned, articulate in their reports, and willing to testify.

The school system set up a review based on its psychiatric exam. They decided Heather was no longer emotionally disturbed but was learning disabled. I went to look at the class for LD children in which they proposed placing her. The class had a male teacher, ten boys, and one girl. I wrote a letter stating that I disagreed with the placement and requested that they postpone a decision until private testing had been completed. They refused.

I received a letter from the board of education saying that it had approved the placement. I called the president of the board and asked his secretary whether the board had been informed that the parent disagreed with the placement and had requested that no decisions be made until private evaluations had been completed. In ten minutes I received a call from the head of special education.

"Why did you call the president of the board?"

"I received a letter from him."

"That's just a form letter. I signed it.'

"I had no way of knowing that."

"I got your letter and I understand your problem with that class. If we set up a meeting in February, will that give you enough time to get the private evaluations completed?"

Neither the teacher nor the assistant principal came to the meeting in February. We gave everyone copies of our reports, and everyone agreed to read them and hold another meeting in March. The psychologist's report called for a therapeutic environment, and the psychiatrist's said that Heather was suffering from Post Traumatic Stress Syndrome and could be suicidal. March came and went. We informed them that they were out of compliance because they hadn't acted on the reports, which they had had for over thirty days.

At the meeting in May they again said they were going to classify Heather LD and place her in that program.

"How will that take care of her emotional needs?"

"You do that privately."

"The psychologist has told you Heather could be suicidal. How are you going to keep her safe?"

"We don't think that . . . "

"You're going to take that chance? I will go on record stating that if anything happens to Heather, or if she hurts another child, I will hold you personally liable."

"You can't do that."

"I can and I will."

"If you don't agree with this, take us to an impartial hearing."

We chose our lawyer, and he called the board of education's lawyer to find out what was going on. He found out that the school system really didn't know where to place Heather because she falls into a lot of categories, and they saw me as overprotective. Another review was decided upon, which both lawyers attended. The lawyer from the board of education commented, "From what I've read and heard here, I wonder how you came up with the LD classification." As a result of the discussion the special-education officers changed Heather's classification to emotionally handicapped and offered to place her in a program for fragile children in a classroom with a twelve-to-one pupil-teacher ratio in a school where there are several EH classes.

"Heather can't function with twelve students to a teacher."

"There'll be an aide."

"You told me that with the last program. I went to visit and there was no aide."

"I don't know where the aide was that day."

"The teacher said she didn't have one."

So Heather has an aide from 8:30 till 3:00, including lunch. We also put on her IEP that she is exempt from school rules, so they can't suspend her. We accepted the program with these modifications.

Terry Sadler, about Heather, ten when placed, fourteen now.

What happened in Heather's case is neither the exception nor the rule. The fact is that a parent advocating for his or her child needs to know the child's rights, the school system's obligations by law, and the process by which to hold the school system accountable. It would be nice to live in a world where parents of children with special needs could expect help to be made readily available, but the fact is that if you don't know who and how to ask, and aren't tenacious in your quest, the child will probably get less than he or she has a right to and you will end up paying more than required. If a book like Osborne's *Complete Legal Guide to Special Education Services* is not available at your library, it is well worth the money. Ask the library to put it on its list for consideration in its next round of purchases.

In securing appropriate education for a special-needs child, the parents must be active participants and have all the facts—for the good of the child and for their own protection. As one parent put it, "I adopted this child to give her a home, not to bankrupt the family."

What All Parents of Handicapped Children Need to Know

1. All children, including mentally, emotionally, and physically handicapped children, have the right to an appropriate education at public expense. Children also have the right to timely testing to determine those needs and the appropriate setting.
2. When a child's educational needs cannot be met in a regular classroom, an Individualized Educational Program (IEP) must be developed and approved by the Committee on Special Education

(CSE) and the parents. If the process is not initiated by the parents, they must be informed and must give permission for the evaluation.

3. If approved, the IEP is implemented immediately. If it is not approved, due process begins immediately.
4. The child remains in his or her present placement until a new IEP is approved.
5. The school system does not have the right to suspend a child on the basis of his or her handicap, and the right of suspension is limited in any case. An emergency or prolonged suspension or outright expulsion requires the convening of the evaluation team to determine the appropriateness of the child's placement.

Mental Health Services

All children adopted when they are older need therapy, some need residential treatment, and a few need hospitalization. Because of the attachment issues, it is important that out-of-home placement be avoided whenever possible. This requires such in-home support as affordable therapy and respite care to prevent parents from burning out and to provide a renewed source of energy and hope for the family. Only when safety becomes the overriding issue is it time for hospitalization or other out-of-home placement.

Therapy

The fact that all children adopted when they are older need therapy is one of the few absolutes in this book. If one thing were to be done to lower the risk for families adopting older children, improve their quality of life, and lower the cost for society, it would be to guarantee these families free and appropriate mental-health care. How can that lower the cost for society? By making it both expected and financially possible for families to have this help when it is needed, costly institutional care can be prevented in many cases. Often now the family keeps trying to manage in the face of overwhelming difficulties until the need has achieved crisis proportions and the hospital or the court has to be involved. Older adopted children need therapy to adjust to the placement, to deal with the finality of placement after finalization, and whenever they recycle their adoption and abuse issues because they have reached a new stage of development. If families don't get therapy when they need it the problems don't go away. Instead, the tension builds.

So, why don't families get therapeutic help? Usually because they can't afford it or, in some cases, can't find it. Some large corporations provide health insurance that includes providing mental-health services. In subsidized adoptions children have Medicaid, but few providers take Medicaid. Psychologists in clinics take Medicaid, but not many are trained in adoption issues or are therapists-in-training, who change every semester and therefore can't provide continuity. If a child's emotional needs are interfering with his or her school performance, that child can receive therapy as part of the IEP, but dealing with adoption issues requires family therapy.

Adoption therapy is different from other child, adult, or family therapy for many reasons. To begin with, the child can't imagine getting better; he or she is only after survival. Survival sometimes requires lying, living in a fantasy world, blaming everyone else for whatever happened, shutting down, keeping secrets, holding everyone who wants to be helpful at bay.

Faced with beginning therapy with an older adopted child and his or her family, a therapist has two choices: sense the strongest emotion in the room and realize that no matter from whom the feeling appears to be coming, its source is the adopted child; or read the child's history of abandonment, abuse, and neglect, ask the parents to describe the behavior they are dealing with, and figure out how the two are connected. The second step in both cases is for the therapist to confront the child with his or her conclusions and proceed as if the child had admitted to feeling that way. Why? By the time most families come to therapy, they are in crisis. There is no time to wait until the child trusts the therapist enough to reveal what is really happening. Relief has to be forthcoming quickly for family preservation and for the safety of the child.

Ken Watson has said that the two first and primary issues for the adoptive family in therapy are validation and relief. The most critical issue for the child is a sense of safety. These must be addressed first and throughout the therapy experience or further work becomes blocked and extremely difficult. For validation, parents need to be affirmed and encouraged. They need to know they are doing the best they can with a hard job and that they will be able to do even better with support. As Adele Hahn put it:

🐾   What I would want from an adoption worker is someone who will advocate for us as human beings trying to do this incredible feat with this little child. I want to be able to talk about how it's really going without being judged and to have it affirmed that this is really hard.
     Adele Hahn, mother of Fred, three when placed, five now.

Talking about how it's really going without fear of being judged brings relief. Parents need the emotional space to let go safely, to vent, and to struggle. Parent groups are great for this, as is therapy. Being given direction and practical strategies to use when dealing with a difficult child is empowering and gives relief. Good therapists for adoptive families know that a large part of their task is supporting the parents in order to enable them to hold on for the length of time it takes the children to make the changes they need to make.

🐾   The year before the adoption was finalized Jess was on Medicaid, which covered counseling, so he was in therapy. It was the "How are you feeling today, Jess?" kind of therapy, which wasn't what he needed. But the therapist did help me with ideas on how to manage Jess. I have a degree in psychology, and I have worked in a private psychiatric hospital, but those experiences didn't help me a whole lot. It was nothing like having Jess in my house. When the adoption was finalized, therapy ended. No more funding.
       Then I came home from town one day to find the sheriff in my driveway. Jess and another kid had broken into a neighbor's house, started a fire, and burned the guy's important papers. When Jess went to court for this destruction of property the court mandated therapy, and we had an excellent therapist from the Evergreen Attachment Center. I liked his directness and confrontation. I think a therapist is good when he faces the kid with what's going on, says it's not acceptable, and deals with it. We did that in the holding therapy, and I needed tools to be able to do that within the family structure.
       Our therapist's belief was that if the parents aren't feeling healthy, well cared for, and taking care of themselves, therapy isn't going to

do the kid any good. So the therapist spent half of his time building me up, assuring me that I was not the cause of this. I lost a lot of guilt at Evergreen. I became very confident in the skills I learned and in myself. Things worked really well until Jess hit seventh grade and stopped cooperating in therapy. Finally the therapist said, "I can't do anymore with him."

Jess became verbally abusive to me and manipulative between me and my husband. We couldn't do anymore with him either, and it got very wearing. We needed respite.

It took the social worker all summer to find a temporary foster family for Jess. Nobody wants a fourteen-year-old behavior problem. The first foster family was very disciplined and kept a close watch on Jess. When they moved, Jess went with a foster family that was convinced we were the problem and that all Jess needed was to emancipate. We met with them every month, and they treated us like garbage. Imagine making an hour's trip every month to be degraded! They didn't think Jess needed any rules, and we kept telling them that he needed more rules and structure than a normal kid. Not until Jess was charged with rape and ran away did they say, "This kid has problems that we are not equipped to handle."

The therapist assigned to Jess during this time was a joke. When Jess ran away the therapist resigned, saying she wasn't cut out for that kind of work. It seemed to us that she was just trying to make a friend. Emotionally disturbed kids don't need somebody to sympathize with them. Then they can keep being victims and don't have to take responsibility for their actions. People making unnecessary allowances because of a child's past prevent them from outgrowing their victimization and becoming healthy individuals.

Charges were pressed, and even though Jess's is a subsidized adoption, Jess wasn't living at home, and he was being cared for by social services 100 percent, our county and the county where he was charged refused to provide him with a lawyer, so we hired one. It made me totally furious that this kid messed up, and I had to pay for it. We settled out of court because I refused to pay more legal fees than were necessary. Jess was charged with three misdemeanors, put on probation for two years, and sent to residential treatment. I thank God for that. Sending him to jail would have been the wrong move.

When Jess was in residential treatment I laid my cards on the table. "I will not be ready for family therapy until Jess has made progress. All we need to do in family therapy is set up the scenario for him to come home."

And when the time came, I said, "Jess, I will never live my life the way it was before, you have to know that. I expect you to have your attitude in check and to be working all the time on staying home and being part of the family. I've worked enough. I've cared more than you have, and there was something wrong with that picture. When you come home, if you start slipping back, you're gone. And don't expect me to bend. I'm standing tall. You live by my rules, or goodbye."

When Jess got out of residential treatment we set him up with a therapist whose office was convenient. He's comfortable to talk to, and I feel support from him. He let me take charge.

"I want to see you first, tell you what happened this week, and how I handled it. Then we can talk about it. Then you talk to Jess afterward. I don't want him coming in and manipulating you, and then having you turn on me." We haven't had any severe problems where the three of us have had to get together at the end.

Kim Brown, about Jess, nine when placed, thirteen now.

Most adoptive parents are very independent people and only go to therapy as a last resort. At that point the family looks as dysfunctional as the child. The unenlightened therapist will consider the parents the problem, treat them, and expect the child to be fine.

🐍 When we first tried to find a therapist for Rob we got two reactions: What's wrong with you that caused this kid's problems? or, What's wrong with you that you want to keep this problem kid? We didn't consider either reaction helpful, so we kept looking.

Natalie and Brady O'Malley, about Rob, eight when placed, twenty-eight now.

🐍 Everybody says, "Dysfunctional kid, dysfunctional family." But adoptive families are different. Older adopted kids have had at least two families, and while the adoptive family may not be ideal, it isn't the family that caused the problem. Parents need a therapist who knows how to deal with that or the kids will bamboozle the daylights out of the therapist.

Elizabeth Packard, mother of a sibling group of three.

When the family members who need support get the blame, the child isn't treated and the situation deteriorates. It's the child's fantasy parents and cognitive distortions that play themselves out in the child's behavior that need to be treated. For this to happen, adoptive parents need to be respected as equal members of the treatment team.

The second respite-care family in the Brown vignette above was allowed to disregard and disrespect the adoptive family to the detriment of the child. A therapeutic respite-care family needs to be supportive of the adoptive family because the purpose of respite care is to support the adoptive parents in their long-term commitment to the child, not to undermine their authority by becoming the fantasy "good" parents or freeing the child from the bondage of his fantasy "bad" parents. Respite-care parents can expect the child to set them up to do one or the other. This is how one parent handled it.

> Phyllis needed a few days respite, so she left Linda with me. At one point Linda said, "I wish you were my mother because we like the same kind of music." I replied, "Your mother is my friend, and she wants to be your mother. I don't."
>
> *Julia Edwards, mother of Maggie and Kelly and support for Phyllis Tate, mother of Linda.*

Adolescents have the most difficult behavior to sort out, and their therapists often get caught in the parent-bashing trap because it's not what the adolescent does but the intensity of the behavior that makes it different from a normal teen acting out.

> When therapists of older adopted children get caught up in adolescent issues, they miss the point. A normal adolescent experiments to see how bad it gets. Jose didn't drink to dabble in alcohol; he drank with a vengeance to be unconscious. When he stayed out it wasn't a day or two to prove his autonomy; he was gone two or three months. A teen might light a tissue in an ashtray to watch it burn. That's quite different from lighting a series of fires. It's an entirely different perspective.
>
> *Elizabeth Packard, about Jose, thirteen when placed, twenty now.*

A therapist who is allied with the adoptive parents can often help them make the most difficult decision of all—that of out-of-home placement. Most adoptive parents don't give up easily, and placing a child out of the home can feel like giving up. Sometimes parents are so involved in the struggle they don't see what it is doing to the rest of the family or to them. They need help to see the danger and think the unthinkable for everyone's sake.

Institutional Care

Institutionalizing a child is a temporary solution of last resort. It becomes necessary when the safety of the child, the family, or both are at risk. Even then it is not an easy thing to do. Some parents look on hospitalization or residential treatment as a phase in the process of the healing that the child needs. For most parents, however, it feels like an admission of failure, like giving up. Children might feel abandoned, angry at being sent away, relieved to have stronger external controls, victorious at leaving their parents before their parents could leave them. No matter what the feelings are, institutionalizing a child interrupts the bonding cycle, and that can have serious consequences. Depending on the effectiveness and length of treatment, institutionalization can be the end of the beginning or the beginning of the end of the child's life in the family.

The most important tasks for the parents at this stage are taking care of themselves and their relationship, taking care of their other children, and continuing to parent the institutionalized child. In the immediate aftermath of such an event parents may feel guilty, relieved, guilty about feeling relieved, angry, discouraged, bewildered, sad. They may blame each other. They may be dismayed to discover that their other children have problems they hadn't noticed before because they were so focused on the child they finally had to institutionalize. It's a bit like the aftermath of a hurricane—devastating. But where there's life there's hope. The pieces can be picked up one at a time.

Older adopted children usually go into placement from their adoptive families when they are in a crisis that requires hospitalization, court action, or both. Experiences with each vary. Some are recounted in other chapters in the book. Two vignettes are given here.

Contrary to what one might think, not all psychiatric hospitals for children are treatment centers; they are crisis-management and diagnostic facilities. When the crisis has been diffused and the diagnosis and recommendation for treatment made, the task of the intake hospital is completed. Those children needing long-term treatment should be discharged into treatment centers or residential schools, if appropriate places in these facilities are available. If not, secure arrangements should be made where they can wait for a bed to become available. Often the adoptive parent will be told, "Your child needs residential treatment, but there is no place available at this time. Please take the child home until a bed becomes available."

If a child needs residential treatment, the child does not belong at home. If the parents think it would be safe to have the child home waiting for an available bed they can agree to that arrangement, but they need to realize that they are agreeing to take responsibility for a child who may (and probably will) revert to old negative behaviors and maybe even escalate them. They also need to realize that they are relieving the system of the pressure to provide the bed. At every stage it is important for parents to know that they have a choice. It is difficult to interface with a system and feel equal, but that is what is necessary. The following vignette shows just how hard it can be.

🗩 Jared did well until he had to change schools for the appropriate fourth-grade program. Toward the end of September his psychiatrist thought Jared needed to be hospitalized, so we took him in. There was an elaborate intake process—taking the whole history and assigning a psychologist, psychiatrist, and social worker. They did real evaluations, came up with good recommendations, provided a safe structure, involved the parents in the decisions about medication. In addition, there was a parent support group and parent-child interactive craft activities. When they were finished, they told us what kind of residential placement Jared needed, that no bed was available at the present time, and that we should take him home until there was.

We said we wouldn't take Jared home until there was a day program for him to go into. We pushed, they pushed, and mysteriously a place opened in the hospital day-school program. The Committee on Special Education (CSE) approved it. Jared did all right at home and in that program until we went on a camping weekend with other families and he got involved in a sexual incident. After that he disintegrated as the summer progressed and became psychotic.

When Jared had been discharged, it was for two months—until a bed in a treatment center became available. Once he was home there was no push to make the bed available, so the June bed wasn't available until July, then August. They asked us to put off residential treatment until October. I said I'd think about it. My wife was furious, so we had a long talk about what was going on. Obviously I had been in denial. When they called and said "Take the bed or lose it," we took it.

In residential care Jared was involved in some sexual incidents and set some fires. Kids assaulted him, and he seemed pleased to be assaulted. His contact with us was minimal, and those we had were slimy. Home passes concerned us because he wasn't really connecting. He commented that he really did well at Thanksgiving because the carving knife was sitting there next to the turkey and he didn't pick it up and stab everybody in the family. That wasn't a comforting comment.

The therapist thought we were the problem, not Jared. When we spoke of the abuse he had suffered, the therapist told Jared he should masturbate rather than interact sexually with the other kids. Jared's response was, "I wanted to do that, but Kevin wouldn't."

We were afraid Jared would abuse our other son, so we set up some criteria. For us to visit Jared, he had to be on level 2 of the hospital behavior mod system; for him to come home, he had to be on level 3.

The therapist agreed but wanted Christmas to be an exception. We didn't want to risk having him home for Christmas. Jared's caseworker gave my wife a hard time. "Only an unfit mother would not want her son home for Christmas." Jared maintained crappy level 1 behavior, and we stood our ground. Meanwhile we kept dealing with the therapist, because we didn't want to give him an excuse to call Child Protective Services and report us as abusive, abandoning parents.

For nine months we visited Jared, even took him off campus if he interacted well. We didn't bring him home, didn't take him on vacation with us. Eventually he began to come around. When it looked like the improvement was consistent, I asked the treatment center to have a packet sent to our school system to prepare for discharge. They refused to let us see the reports or to send them. They had approval for Jared until the end of the school year and were determined he wouldn't go home until then because they would lose the funding. We tried all the channels we could, to no avail.

Eventually his placement in school was prepared and he had an entry date. The weekend before this Jared was home on a pass, and we simply did not return him to the center. We gave twenty-four-hour notification that we were removing him. They didn't fight it; they discharged him. He has been doing fine ever since.

Craig Clark, about Jared, four when placed, twelve now.

This vignette brings out three important points: the child communicates by action as well as words, parents have to stay in charge and be persistent, and systems have to work together.

When dealing with children in this situation it is important to take their behavior seriously. Their behavior is their most reliable form of communication. I am sure that if the therapist had asked Jared if he wanted to go home for Christmas, he would have said yes. He might have wanted to go, or to answer what the therapist wanted to hear, but he didn't feel safe going. By staying on level 1 he made sure he couldn't go, and thus he kept himself and his family safe. If the child's words and actions contradict each other, it is safer to believe the actions. Because therapy is usually a verbal exchange, therapists are in danger of getting caught up in the words. This makes them vulnerable to manipulation.

The adoptive parents are the permanent members of the child's treatment team, know the child well, orchestrate transitions, and, if all goes well, will be living with the results of the treatment. The professionals are experts in their fields. The parents are the experts on the child. It is not that the parents are always right, but their opinions need to be considered seriously. "Fix the family and you've fixed the child" does not apply to older child adoption, because as crazy as the family might look by the time the child is hospitalized, it is not the family that caused the problem. It's the family that is invested in being the solution. If the child is to return to the family after treatment, the family needs to be supported, respected, and involved in the treatment process.

Treatment usually starts with hospitalization or a court appearance, after which one of three types of residential placement might be recommended. The most typical is the residential school, a placement that usually will be made through the office of special education of the local school district. The hospital may then prepare a packet of materials regarding the child and the school district sends the packets out. Schools contacted that think their program meets the child's needs—and that will have a bed in the near future—then set up an interview. If the child is refused everywhere he or she has an interview, or gets no interviews, then the school system can send the applications to contracted schools out of state and the hospital can send them to the office of mental health for a placement in a residential treatment facility. These are the options if the hospital is the child's entry point in the treatment loop.

If the court is the entry point, the child may be able to be placed through the school district or the Department of Social Services (DSS). If the child is to be placed through DSS, the parent usually will have to sign a paper giving DSS custody during the time of placement. This makes parents feel as though they have disrupted the adoption and the children feel they have been abandoned again. It weakens the parents' position on the treatment team and complicates the therapy. Parents are usually required to pay a percentage of their income for the placement unless the adoption has been subsidized from the beginning. Sometimes parents are asked to foot the entire bill.

🖝   When David first went to the hospital we billed our company insurance plan. It was used up in one month, so the hospital picked up with Medicaid. When the court sent David to a residential treatment facility, we were asked to pay 10 percent of our income for David's treatment. They took it right out of our salary. The people at work were alarmed. It's a big chunk of money, and we still have his three sisters at home. But David's getting what he needs, and that's the important thing.

Joy and Bud Zack, about David, twelve when placed, eighteen now.

Even when the adoption has been subsidized from the beginning, payment can be an issue. This chapter will end with the story of the Walker family, because their case shows the interplay of all three systems.

❧ Dolores was placed with me in October, when she was twelve. In September of the following year she began running away regularly and being gone for a week at a time. In desperation I took out a PINS (Person in Need of Supervision) petition on her. Before the court action had been completed, Dolores's therapist decided that she needed to be hospitalized, so she was placed in a children's psychiatric center.

After three months the center decided to discharge her. We had not had a successful home visit, she had been on behavioral level 0 for twenty-eight days straight, yet the plan was to send her home. I insisted that they discharge her to the court because of the PINS petition, and the court sent her to an adolescent shelter where she lived for the next seven months when she was not on run away.

Meanwhile, the school system sent out packets of her material to all the appropriate residential schools; she was refused everywhere. Dolores had set two fires when she was in the crisis unit, so she was a high-risk applicant. Finally her application was sent to the Department of Mental Health for placement in a residential treatment facility. The Department of Mental Health didn't think she required that level of care. I appealed the decision on the grounds that she had been rejected at all possible less restrictive placements. The Department of Mental Health reconsidered and set up an interview. Dolores missed the interview because she was AWOL from the shelter. "You missed the bed. There won't be another one available for two months." I was frantic because her running away activity was so high risk that I didn't think she would still be alive then.

I applied for private placement in a facility in another state. Dolores was accepted on the basis of a video taken during a therapy group in which she had participated. The court agreed to the placement, provided I would pay for it. Meanwhile, several days before we were to leave, Dolores was found barefoot in the slush on a corner in a very dangerous section of town at 5:30 in the morning. She had tied her sheets together at 2 A.M. and gone out the window of the shelter in a sleet storm. "This is suicidal activity," I said to the social worker. "Please hospitalize her for the next few days so she doesn't miss the plane." They did, and she finally got into treatment.

The Department of Social Services canceled Dolores's subsidy because she wasn't living with me. I was paying for private placement and the subsidy would have paid for two days of treatment per month and provided Medicaid. I got a lawyer and called for a fair hearing. The adoption agency provided me with the 1985 wording of the law in my state that won the day. In my state the child has to be supported by the parent, not necessarily living at home, to continue the subsidy after placement. The Department of Social Services felt that if I could pay for private placement I didn't need the subsidy, and for a long time I thought that too. The representative of the adoption agency clarified that issue for me: "It isn't yours to need. Dolores has a right to it." The subsidy kept coming until she was twenty one. I used it to pay her rent to her landlord after she was eighteen. This helped her out and kept us in touch.

When I adopted a second child, aged thirteen, I refused to take her without a subsidy, without Medicaid. For two and a half years the Medicaid card came monthly and the placement went well. After we finalized a few checks came, less than one hundred dollars each. Eventually I received a letter asking for an income statement from me. I didn't answer the letter because the placement was going so well. I knew the subsidy was not based on my income but on her being thirteen at the time of the adoption and therefore hard to place. Because I didn't answer the letter, the subsidy was forever canceled.

Several months later Clara stopped working in therapy, began to disintegrate, threatened to kill us, and had to be placed in a residential school. Without the subsidy I had to pay 17 percent of my income for the placement. Had I answered that letter, her state of origin would have been billed. Not answering that letter was a very expensive mistake. Never adopt an older child without a subsidy, and never let the subsidy lapse no matter how well things are going. You never know what's ahead, and you need to stay prepared and financially protected.

Hope Walker, about Dolores, twelve when placed, nineteen now, and Clara, thirteen when placed, eighteen now.

9

A Family
That Transcends Expectations

Each family member has expectations, and society has expectations of the family. We make decisions depending on what we expect to happen as a result. We are judged on how we meet other people's expectations. Fidelity often requires that we transcend our expectations of ourselves, others, and situations. This in turn requires adaptation and growth. Courage is required to change and grow in a way that doesn't fit other people's expectations. A byproduct of an adoptive family's way of meeting everyone's needs often is its becoming somehow unique. In the process, expectations of the members change and the family changes in unexpected ways.

To begin with, parents have to give up the expectation that the children will be like them. Most parents go through this when their child goes through adolescence, but the parents of older adopted children deal with it from the end of the honeymoon period. One parent put it this way:

❧ Intentionally building an adoptive family is a process that never ends. You just keep working through a series of crises, and change comes in the aftermath. The first crisis is testing, and it comes within the first few months. Jose ran away a few times, so I was feeling this kid doesn't like me. I was fighting all the way. "Come on now, let's get with the program. Shape up." I wanted them to forget where they'd come from and who they were.

The children desperately wanted somebody to love them, and they wanted to stay together as a family. My wife and I desperately wanted to have kids and wanted them to love us. For a while we felt we were being rejected and it really hurt. Eventually we began to realize that we were not really being rejected. We were being confronted with a life that already existed. We needed to nurture it, but we could not control it. We needed to stop expecting that the kids would reject their old values and accept ours. We needed to help them identify and affirm their positive strengths, as well as blend the old and the new. We hope eventually they will develop a coherent positive stance toward life based on surviving losses and not being afraid of them.

Egan Packard, parent of a sibling group of three.

One expectation the children have that needs to be transcended is that it is only a matter of time until they will have to leave. This is an insidious belief that recurs with particular vengeance when finalization is imminent. But it also is likely to surface when a family moves—"We're not all going. You're going to leave us"—when parents go on a childless vacation—"You'll never come back"—when another child joins the family—"He's here to replace me." It even comes into play sometimes when guests come to dinner and the child thinks he or she is being looked over by another set of possible parents. Its root is in the fear of abandonment and the child's conviction that he or she isn't good enough. Even Janet, whose story is featured below, and who had shown great trust and a consistent desire to belong to her adoptive family, was not free of this expectation.

✦ Janet had been in our home for about six months when she was five, then went back to her birth family, then into foster care with another family, then home again. We kept in touch through the years. One day Janet called us and said, "I've had all I can take of this abuse. I will report it if you promise me that I can come to your house. I can't do this without somebody I know." In reporting the abuse Janet took a risk that most children couldn't take, and that has made her a survivor. She came to live with us around her fourteenth birthday.

Janet kept saying she wanted to belong here, to have only one set of parents to go to for permissions. We kept asking the social worker, the attorney advocate, and the birth mother to sit down with us and plan for Janet's future.

The social worker said, "This kid doesn't need a permanent home because in two years she is going to be gone anyway."

One night Janet's birth mother called asking if she could bring Janet a birthday present. She came, we all had dinner together, and afterward we put the youngest kids to bed, sent her son and mine downstairs to play Nintendo, and until 2:30 in the morning worked out an agreement with the birth mother and Janet about Janet's future. At the next foster care review the birth mother announced that she had decided to terminate her parental rights. We waited the requisite thirty days and filed our petition to adopt.

While we were waiting for finalization, Janet exhibited fears that we were going to send her away. It was the self-fulfilling childhood fantasy—I can only be so good for so long and they're eventually going to send me away, so why not be bad so they can get it over with? We spent time explaining to her that we loved her, but we didn't particularly like some of her actions. There was nothing she could do that would make us not her parents, but some of the things she was doing could jeopardize her placement without our having any say in the matter. For example, she drove her grandmother's car alone, out of state, without a license. She didn't get caught, but we pulled her permit. "Since you are now a good enough driver that you don't need adult supervision, and a permit is for practice, you don't need it any more." The world revolved around her getting her license on her sixteenth birthday. We also grounded her for thirty days. If we went someplace, she was invited or told to come along. There were no sleepovers, no going to friends' houses.

We finalized her adoption and Randy's on June 7. All the kids and Janet's best friend since fourth grade went with us to the ceremony. I think Janet expected fireworks, the world to be lifted off her shoulders, and the sun to come out and shine. The next day was just the next day, and she was almost depressed. She hadn't expected to feel the severance. She had to do some work to let go of her birth mother and her anger at her. We did a lot of talking and crying on the back porch.

On June 16, her sixteenth birthday, we wrapped her permit up and returned it to her. She got her license a week later.

Chad and Amy Bowers, about Janet, fourteen when placed, seventeen now.

Sometimes parents have to give up expectations of themselves. We all have certain standards to which we hold ourselves, but these need to be modified to meet different and more challenging situations. If not, the very stress they create can jeopardize our chance of success, if for no other reason than they wear us out and misdirect our focus.

🌿 I am a perfectionist. I try to be a perfect wife, perfect mother, perfect secretary. Life with Dennis got really difficult. One morning when I got to the office I began crying hysterically and couldn't stop. Thank goodness no one was there. I called the psychologist and said, "I've got to see you. I don't know how long I can hold on." He canceled an appointment and saw me. I was in knots.

"Say, I want to get rid of Dennis," he said.

"No, I don't."

"Just say it."

"I want to get rid of Dennis."

"Louder."

"I want to get rid of Dennis."

"Say it like you mean it!"

"I WANT TO GET RID OF DENNIS!"

It was the weirdest thing. Every time I said it, it was as if tons of weight fell off my shoulders. The therapist said, "It doesn't hurt you to say it. You are not going to get rid of him, but you have to accept the fact that you have a hard time handling it any more."

I thought I was the most horrible person in the world to think of getting rid of this little boy who had no place to go. On the other hand, it *was* hard, and all I had to do was admit it. After that I loved Dennis all to pieces again.

Darlene Olson, about Dennis, seven when placed, sixteen now.

Couples need to let go of the expectations they have of the outcome. Instead of focusing on making things happen, it is often necessary to help them unfold, to see the way the wind is blowing and change course, to bend and always take care of each other so that neither breaks. Structure is important, but rigidity has no place in older child adoption.

🌿 When we were being prepared to adopt, the adoption worker said to us, "The biggest problem you two have is you're both winners." After a year of parenting I understood what he meant. The effort doesn't produce the rewards you expect with the kids. What he missed with us was our level of commitment. If we can't get a win the conventional way, we'll find other ways to make it work or change our expectations of what a "win" is.

We expected the kids to be traumatized, that we'd have a year of hell, then we'd finally be accepted. That was naive. The kids drag their baggage along with them, constantly revisiting it in various ways in the different stages of their lives. And they use us as surrogate punching bags to get rid of their frustration.

When we were new parents we had to learn how to punish in a way that made sense. They taunted us: "What are you going to do? Make me stand in a corner with my feet spread out against the wall? Beat me with a belt?" At first we said, "Absolutely under no circumstances are we going to spank you." We warned, talked, gave choices. We'd put them in time-out in a chair in the hall, and if it was a long time-out we'd give them books. They'd break the chair, pull their socks apart, throw the books on the floor, smash the wall. Sometimes we had to hold on to Barry to keep him in the chair. We finally said, "We'll give you one whack in the butt, that's it." Strangely enough that calmed them down. They understood it, and there was a limit on it so we didn't get abusive. Because I couldn't spank I'd say, "The hand of Mom," and my husband would deliver the whack on my behalf. It solidified us marvelously, but we were exhausted all the time, and we occasionally overreacted. Jared squirted water in my face, and I slapped him hard on the shoulder. I didn't like myself afterward. Fortunately in therapy we were learning techniques to diffuse the anger. Within a year we decided it wasn't working. We had to make a change.

Because of where our jobs were at the time, and because the boys were really going after the person called Mommy, my husband, Craig, gave up his job and became an at-home parent. He's home all day, I go out to work, and we're finding that the arrangement stretches us as people. Craig is involved in the day-to-day worries and long-term observation. I walk in the door in the evening and say, "Wait a minute, this is nuts" or "Hey, this is working well" because I have a fresh look at it. I get to be the reward person on the weekends. It's not gender oriented, it's occupational.

My husband and I both come from good families, but we've both had to have individual therapy to cope with what comes up with the children. In school I was a brilliant student, and whenever

I wasn't successful I just ducked into something else. I ran away from my problems. What I'm gaining from this is the ability to be consistent, not to duck out when things get uncomfortable, but to see life as a river pulsing along. And I have a much more comfortable feel for where my husband is in terms of our marriage. I know he's there, I know how strong he is, and I know how much he loves me and the family.

We continued to put a lot of energy into parenting and were continually faced with the terrible damage sexual abuse had done to the boys. I don't think Barry was sure whether he was a girl or a boy. Jared felt crazy and talked about needing hospitalization. He dismantled things and started collecting sharp objects. They both have intense unresolved anger and core trust issues they haven't gotten past. Eventually they were both hospitalized.

We took an out-of-season vacation. I couldn't get out of bed for two weeks. We'd wake up at 2:00 A.M., 4:00 A.M., sleep all day. We were blown away by the possibility that neither of the boys would be able to survive to adulthood in a sane manner. Eventually we pulled ourselves back together and one at a time, little by little, so did the boys. Jared started making progress and coming home for visits. Barry still had only a mattress in his room at the hospital and someone watching him every minute of the day.

Then one day my husband agreed that we would provide respite care for a child whose adoption was disrupting. The child arrived the Saturday that my husband was going out with some friends. I told Ray he could call us Mr. and Mrs. Clark, we got him settled, and my husband left for the day. This was a kid who was sweet, quiet, just wanted to sit and watch Mr. Rogers. When my husband got home at eleven that night I was waiting up, ready to punch him. He looked at me and said, "This is not about me. I'm going to get out of here till you calm down, then we'll talk."

Eventually he made tea and I went through every emotion in the book. Finally I said, "Ray's an adorable kid. He's got problems, but they're not so bad. How come we can't have him? How come we couldn't have a kid who could give something back, who could make it? Ray's not so bad and his parents are allowed to disrupt, and I can't disrupt from my kids who are in the hospital because you have this commitment and you won't let me. Why can't I have a kid like Ray? What's wrong with me?"

My husband listened to my raving sympathetically.

Eventually I ended with, "Let's adopt Ray. His behaviors are outrageous, but they don't require hospitalization."

Jared came home on a pass and said, "Doesn't this kid have parents? Maybe we should give him a home."

We told the social worker, "If Ray gets placed with another rookie family he'll blow out again. I think we can work with him and he's more likely to be comfortable in our house where he's not going to stick out like a sore thumb."

The adoption worker agreed and we told Ray he could call us Mom and Dad. Then we introduced our family to each other in the controlled environment of the hospital waiting room.

On his passes Jared was confronted by the fact that we were telling Ray the same things we had told him. Ray was doing what he was told, and we were following through as we said we would. Jared started realizing that we were trustworthy. We had been very consistent with him and Barry for years, but they had never believed us. Barry and Jared realized that they better get their act together. Ray was showing Jared who was showing Barry the path home.

Craig and Mitzi Clark, about Barry, Jared, and Raymond, three, four, and six when placed, eleven, twelve, and ten now.

One thing it is reasonable to expect when you adopt an older child is that it will be a challenge in ways you cannot imagine ahead of time. If you are a confident person, you also expect you will be able to handle whatever happens. But everyone has an Achilles' heel and older adopted children have a way of finding it with uncanny accuracy. When this happens it is important to expect that you will find the help you need from each other and in the larger community rather than that you will be able to handle it all on your own. Better to go into therapy, heal hurts previously forgotten, and grow, than to wall yourself up for survival. The payback for most adoptive parents isn't that they have recreated the Walton family, but that they have salvaged kids who might have been lost, learned to support each other creatively, and grown in unexpected ways.

❧ Sometimes I give and give and give and feel there's nothing left. Then my husband will walk up to me and say, "Stop, right now.

You need a hug. Now stand still and let me give it to you." He'll
set the timer for sixty seconds, hug me and make me hug him back
without stirring a pot, without patting a kid's head. I've done the
same for him, and the kids are picking up on it. While Daddy is on
the road the two older ones will say, "Momma, you're getting crazy
again. Can I give you a hug?"

We had been taking two adults-only trips a year, one in the win-
ter for business and a long weekend in the summer for our anniversary, but we haven't gone anywhere this year. We still work well
together, but we haven't taken enough time to play together. We
will occasionally pull rank on our oldest and say, "I'm sorry if you've
got plans tonight. Your friends are welcome to come to the house
but we've got to get away." Sometimes we'll get up early, forbid
the kids to come out on the back porch, and sit there with a cup of
coffee, just the two of us. We take showers together almost daily,
because that's the one time we can talk and generally not be disturbed. We also have a motorcycle that will seat only two people,
and we can take a ride on a beautiful summer night. We tell the
kids that the only way we can take good care of them is to take
good care of ourselves.

Chad and Amy Bowers, parents of five older adopted children.

   When I started therapy with Dolores our therapist said to me, "This
is a very passionate little girl. If her passion ever opens up you are
not going to be able to handle it." With his help I've become a lot
warmer. I have learned to feel my feelings as I go along. I can show
Curt how sad I am that things aren't the way they could be with us.

Instead of playing the Lone Ranger I have learned to reach out
for help when I need it, when everything gets too big for me. Since
I became an adoptive parent I've made a lot of friends and felt the
most alive I've ever felt. When we weren't in crisis I even enjoyed
the everyday challenge of getting the behavior that was necessary
in a given situation without getting into a control battle. At our
support group meetings we joked a lot, "Oh, for a boring day!"

Hope Walker, single parent of three children.

And finally, couples have to let go of expecting life ever to be as it
once was. Adoption isn't a matter of a kid fitting in. Everything and
everyone will be stretched in the process of making a fit. Certainly all

families adjust when there's a new baby, but that is not the same as welcoming and beginning the process of taming an unkempt and angry three year old.

❦ *Mom:* When we met Fred he didn't tug at my heartstrings at all, he was such a little macho thing. He had an old face, a gray pallor, and dark circles from poor nutrition. I had wanted to be a mom, wanted a baby for so many years, and here's Fred, not a baby, not cuddly, not even a regular three year old.

Dad: I was immediately attracted to Fred.

Mom: Two weeks after we got Fred, I got accepted into graduate school. It seemed as though I was going to have to choose between my two adult aspirations: going to graduate school and being a mom. It had been really hard getting into graduate school, and we had made a major shift in lifestyle to get here. If we left, we were never coming back. I realized that if I stayed home with Fred and he continued to act as badly as he was acting, I was going to be one angry mother and that wasn't going to be good, so I decided to go to school and somehow it would all work out.

Dad: Early on I thought, while my wife is going to school, I'm going to be there for Fred. It's a great sense of accomplishment, the greatest I've had, just making it work and gearing the time, the love, and the effort.

Mom and Dad: We had been together for ten years. We had always said whatever needed to be said, screamed, yelled, cried, then kissed and made up and everything was fine. When we'd do that when Fred was around he'd freak out, start banging his head and running around making noises. We used to be able to lie in bed in the morning and do whatever we needed to do to get connected and be intimate. Now Fred's in there as soon as he's up. All the superficial aspects of living get thrown into the fire when you adopt a child.

Mom: I'll hear Fred talking to my husband the way I do when I get on him about things. I'll say, "Don't be disrespectful." Then I think, no wonder he's saying these things. I am more aware of the way I treat my husband because I don't want Fred to relate to his father that way.

Fred has also helped me discover the angry part of me, face it, embrace it, and try to deal with it. I have PMS and if I drink coffee, hit my cycle, and have to deal with Fred, I will get violent. It starts a cycle that can last a week or two. Fred is this growing, thriving human being, and I just can't be thrashing through this. I've got to rid myself of the things that are harmful to him.

Dad: Having Fred has made me understand a lot about my own childhood. I had never spent time thinking about those parts of it that having him, and seeing my behavior in response to him, bring up. Learning more about life, what love is, what works, what doesn't work, is as valuable to me and us as it is to him.

Mom and Dad: We both have a deep life-long commitment to growing as people in the circumstances we create, or as our past experiences re-create them. In the past two years we've both had to let go of the resistance we've had to the changes we've made, and those which have come about because we adopted Fred. We've both had to replace the resistance with giving ourselves to this marriage and the adoption to make it all work.

Aaron and Adelle Hahn, parents of Fred, three when placed, five now.

Because there is such an overwhelming challenge involved, it is risky to begin an older child adoption with one member of the couple having reservations. Because Fred's dad was able to take on the major portion of the child care in the beginning, and his mom went to graduate school, neither felt deprived of life aspirations during the adjustment period, and eventually Fred was able to tiptoe into both their hearts. This arrangement stretched them financially, but that was a stretch they could handle.

While two couples, the Clarks and the Hahns, found it necessary to reverse roles to make their adoptions work, the Bowers also made an unusual adjustment.

❥ The job had me on the road a lot. Life at home deteriorated with the children acting out, fussing, and fighting among themselves. Everyone was worn out all the time, and I just drifted through on weekends. We own a small business, and we decided that we could make it if I came in off the road, so I quit a good paying job to spend more time with my family. Now I work at night and have the kids in the day during the week, and my wife works during the day and has them in the evening. Having a family-owned business we can do that and save all the child-care expenses.

Amy and Chad Bowers, parents of five older children, adopted separately.

When a couple focuses on the family and is flexible about the "givens," it can evolve into something unusual but workable and satisfying. In the long run that's what matters.

What enables a family to transcend expectations? There is either something enlivening within the situation that enables family members to plod on into uncharted territory, or there is a strength that comes from without. The enlivening factor is different for each parent.

❧ I get angry at Josh because he challenges everything I say. When I ask him not to do something, he'll do it over and over again. I feel drained by him, so I need respite. I need time to catch my breath and pump myself up so I can take some more when he comes home, but when I am away from him I can hardly wait to get back and see what he's doing. He tries hard and does the impossible.

I bought Josh a tricycle. When I told his physical therapist she said, "He cannot ride it because he cannot do side-to-side motion yet." Within three months Josh was riding, pedaling forward and backward. He does things like this all the time, and it's exciting.

Judy Doggart, about Josh, two when placed, nine now.

❧ Casey and I were driving somewhere one day and we saw a dog limping along the side of the road.

"Stop, we've got to pick up the dog."

"We're late for our appointment. We can't stop. The dog is obviously not lost. He's limping, but he's probably going home."

"We've got to stop and pick him up," Casey said, and started crying. "She took care of the owls, the badgers, and the foxes but she couldn't take care of me. She gave me away. Stop and pick up the dog."

His mother had a wild animal handler's permit. All the wounded badgers, skunks, and foxes went to her house to be cured. How could I turn him away after that?

Earl Raleigh, about Casey, thirteen when placed, eighteen now.

🌿 Did you ever see the movie *Somewhere in Time?* The first time Hillary heard the story and asked about it I said, "Yes, we all have a spirit, and our spirit is perfect. Hillary's spirit has hands. Theo's has perfect feet that don't hurt when he walks. Teresa's doesn't have all those burn scars. Here we all have problems with our physical bodies, but our spirits are perfect."

Later, when they were getting ready for bed, Hillary asked, "You're not lying to me?"

"About what?"

"My spirit has hands?"

"No, I'm not lying to you. Your spirit has hands."

"What color are they?"

"The same color as your feet. And your spirit hands are beautiful like Renee's." Hillary was almost floating.

Sometimes when Derek is having one of his screaming fits, or Theo is in terrible pain after surgery, I just want to throw this all in. Then I have to remember that their spirits know no handicap. Derek's spirit has no emotional problems, Theo's spirit has beautiful feet, Hillary's spirit has arms.

I have to focus on what's really inside. When I see my children, I see what really could be there. Whether they ever become that is their choice.

Shirley Newman, birth parent and adoptive parent of older children from the foster-care system and other countries.

🌿 There's a lot of talk about social justice and saving the world. It's been very important for me to have this family to make a statement about racism and to love these particular individuals.

There's a lot of growth that comes from interacting with these kids. I've learned how to give without getting something back. I give, and there are times like Mother's Day when I expect a return. I went three Mother's Days without getting a card. Then I asked myself, "Are you doing all this just to get cards on Mother's Day?" I came to terms with it and kept on, knowing that it might take a few years. Last year, for the first time, Kerry gave me a card. I was really excited!

There is satisfaction in seeing the kids change. When Lucille came, the school system wanted to put her in special education because she was three grades behind. But she got all the way through and it was great to see her graduate from eighth grade.

At a family gathering recently people came up to us and commented about how wonderfully the children have turned out, how personable they are. It bowled us over, and we realized the three of them have come a long way, that maybe we have done something.

Edsel and Marcia Dean, parents of three children adopted when they were older.

Life, relationships, and family are the biggest challenge for some people and they are as enlivened (and as spent) by meeting that challenge as a climber is in conquering Mount Everest or a CEO in heading a Fortune 500 company. Life in the family of an older adopted child is like an Apollo 13 mission. You start out wanting to walk on the moon and you end up being as creative as possible in landing your vehicle safely.

Parents learn to accept what their children can give and tenaciously hold on to this half-filled cup. If a child can't or won't give anything back, parents get what they need from another source. And, of course, it never hurts to have a sense of humor.

❧ Now I have one twenty-one year old, and seven between the ages of thirteen and nineteen. I thought that when my kids were teenagers I'd have more time. No. When your kids are teenagers, be at home. I'm amazed at what they can do in a few hours when I'm not there. If I'm off to a meeting they can go to a party and be back before I am.

"You didn't tell me I couldn't go."

"No parties during the week, remember?"

There is also no TV during the week, and no violent videos or adult or R-rated movies at any time.

"I can see them," they tell me.

"Not in my house," I respond. A couple of years ago I was taking them all to see *Back to the Future III*. We were in line and the theater was also showing *Robocop II* and *Diehard II*. They decided to embarrass me.

"Mom, get off it. Why aren't we going to see these other movies?" said one.

"Think about it, Mom, sooner or later we are going to see *Die-hard II*, so why not tonight?" said another.

"Sooner or later you are going to have sex, too, but I am not taking you to a brothel tonight," I replied, exasperated.

"Why didn't you say it a little louder? Everybody's looking at us!"

Without further argument we saw *Back to the Future III*. They always push me, and if they can push me in public, all the better. They may see *Diehard II* tomorrow somewhere else, but the fact that they know I consider it unacceptable is going to have some bearing on their personality somewhere down the line.

May Udall, single parent of four children adopted as babies and four adopted when they were older.

Conclusions

There are two main conclusions to which the material in this book leads. The first is that a consistent, loving caregiver belongs on the list of a child's basic needs along with food, clothing, and shelter. The second is that families who adopt older children need therapeutic support services that far surpass those provided to families adopting babies. Unfortunately these services, when they exist at all, are woefully inadequate.

Supportive services for young, first-time, high-risk birth parents are of utmost importance, because it is best for children to remain with their birth parents whenever possible. Once out-of-home placement has occurred, the best interest of the child continues to be a permanent, loving home in which to grow. This means either returning to a strengthened birth family or moving into the permanence of adoption in a reasonable amount of time with as few foster families as possible in the interim.

Regardless of the conditions of the birth home, being removed from it is traumatic for the child. That move and every move thereafter weakens the child's ability to attach. Children who have trusted and attached once can transfer that trust and attach again, but they cannot do this indefinitely. It is therefore imperative that permanent placement for the child be achieved with the fewest possible moves.

Of the eight children in the sample who were adopted by their first or second foster parents, only one required placement out of the adoptive home. This is a far cry from the Walker family where, according to the children's histories, Hope Walker was mother number five for Dolores, who had been in foster care for eight years; number twelve for Clara, who had been in care eleven years; and number seven for Curt, who spent three years in foster care. All three children were attachment disordered, and all three required long-term placement out of the adoptive home.

In a conversation with his adoptive mother Curt put it this way: "I have mommaphobia."

"What's that?"

"It's when you've had the same mother for five years and you love her."

An attachment-disordered child loves and is phobic about loving, and therein lies the agony. Living in the push-pull relationship that this creates tears everyone apart. Some children enter the system attachment disordered. Those who don't, but have multiple placements in care, often become attachment disordered. Therefore it is necessary to create a system that prevents multiple foster placements. This requires abiding by the time limits established by law and realistic long-term planning from the beginning of placement.

In some states the law gives birth parents twelve months to prove their capability and intent to make the changes necessary to be able to parent their children. Some state laws give those who have foster-parented the children the right to adopt them once their birth parents' rights have been relinquished or terminated. So why do children spend so long in foster care? And why are many not adopted by their foster parents?

Of course there is a reluctance to terminate parental rights because it is a serious step. But isn't leaving the child in foster care also serious? It is reasonable to think that some foster parents would hold back their feelings and commitment to the child in order to protect themselves from the hurt of eventually losing the child. The longer a child is in a foster home, the more likely that child is to attach and the more hurtful will be the move to an adoptive or another foster home. The longer a child is in foster care, the more moves he or she is likely to have. The more moves, the more damage.

The present system places children on an emergency basis in the most appropriate foster home with an available bed. Because *availability* is the key word, the fit between the child's needs and the family's resources may be poor. The child stays there until he or she is either returned to the birth home, moves from emergency care to a more long-term foster family, moves to another foster family for another reason, or is adopted.

When children return home and it doesn't work out, they have to be returned to foster care. Usually little effort is made to place them with the foster parents they already know. They just move on. This provides no sense of continuity and doesn't take into account the children's attachment needs.

Could there be several levels of foster care? What if a child entered foster care spending a maximum of thirty days in a home with Mr. and Mrs. X while a long-term plan is made? If, given the history, the chances are good that the birth family will be able to make the changes necessary to parent the child safely, the child could be placed with foster parents trained to care for the child and foster the development of a healthy relationship with the birth parents. If there is very little chance that the birth parents will be able to make the necessary changes, the child could be placed in at risk pre-adoptive placement (*at-risk* because the child is placed before the termination of parental rights; *pre-adoptive* because the foster parents commit to adopting the child if the parents are unable to make the necessary progress in the allotted time). The foster-care system needs to provide children not only with food and shelter but also with the consistency in caregivers that builds trust and preserves the child's ability to attach. This is happening in some parts of the country already.

Even though special-needs adoptions began to get increased attention in the 1960s, before 1980 most adoptions were infant adoptions. Most children who had been removed from their families because of abandonment, neglect, or abuse lived in foster families until their birth families made the changes necessary to have them returned or until they reached the age of eighteen. Since 1980, the availability of abortion, society's growing acceptance of single parents, and the Family Preservation Act of 1980 have aged the face of adoption. The Family Preservation Act proclaimed the right to a permanent home for all children, including those in foster care, at a time when fewer babies were available. Children who had previously been considered unadoptable began to be adopted. Agencies continued to provide the same support they had always provided for adoptive families—an account of the child's history with the names deleted, a monthly supervisory visit until the court finalized the adoption, and an amended birth certificate afterward.

When the child's history includes not simply the parent's age and condition at the time of the baby's relinquishment at birth but a history of the child's neglect, abuse, and multiple moves, this isn't enough support. In some states the foster-care system recognizes this and provides foster children with therapy and foster parents with respite care and support groups. These same services need to be uniformly available and continued during pre-adoptive placement and beyond finalization. These services are expensive, and unless it is a subsidized

adoption the state does not provide them after the adoption is finalized. Children adopted when they are older need to have a subsidy
that provides ongoing treatment as a matter of course.

Timely services of sufficient intensity to prevent parent burn out
and placement out of the adoptive home are as necessary in adoption
as in foster care. It makes no sense for a child to be removed from an
adoptive home to a therapeutic foster home. The adoptive home needs
the services to itself be therapeutic. Except in the case of danger to the
child or others, removals are to be avoided because they damage the
ability of the child to trust and attach. If the state needs to pay as much
to keep the child in the home as it would to keep the child in residential treatment, it is still money well spent to preserve the bond that is
forming. Children who can work through their grief, rage, and abuse—
and learn to give and receive love and to take responsibility for their
actions in a family—develop a conscience and become productive members of society. Money will not need to be spent to protect society from
them when they are adults.

In spite of the difficulties, there are families willing and able to commit to these children permanently. These families deserve to be considered part of society's treatment team for the re-parenting of those children whose birth families could not provide a safe environment for
them. Such adoptive parents need to be trusted with the child's full
history and have free access to the training and services necessary to
provide a therapeutic family setting. When these services are not provided free of charge, the child remains in the home without services
because the family cannot afford them until the situation is irreparable
and out-of-home placement is the only option. Out-of-home placement is the most expensive and least effective form of treatment in
both emotional and financial terms. Regrettably, it is sometimes necessary. But when it can be prevented by timely and intense intervention,
this is the most cost-effective plan. The problem is, there isn't a plan;
there is only a budget

✍ *Parent:* "You're going to spend the rest of his life paying to support him if you don't give me the right help for him now."
  Social Worker: "We can't worry about what's going to happen down
  the road, our budget's really tight this year."
  Ida Aldez, single parent of Darcy.

❧ Sometimes you look at the headlines and a whole town is galvanized because a little girl has fallen in a well and will spend whatever it takes to get her out. We have thousands of throw-away kids. It's heartbreaking. They deserve a chance.

Earl Raleigh, single parent of Casey.

It is hard to imagine anyone standing at the mouth of the well, looking at the little girl and feeling OK about the fact that there is no rescue equipment to call. The social worker quoted above is saying either that there isn't any, or that what there is is used to capacity elsewhere.

The older adopted child is the child in the well. The families who respond are the rescue workers. The vignettes in this book afford a rare view of the process as it takes place in the privacy of adoptive families' homes and hearts. These are the children and families who deserve a leg up. They need therapists trained in the treatment of children with adoption and abuse issues, supportive respite care, and, as a last resort, treatment centers where children can work through the difficult feelings they cannot work through safely at home. Unfortunately, the availability of appropriate mental-health services for families is woefully inadequate. Developing them requires more than a budget. It requires an investment, one which is long overdue.

Couples who have a chronically or terminally ill child have a very high divorce rate. The extreme financial stress of such a trauma can tear parents apart in their grieving. In many ways parenting an older adopted child can bring similar stresses. It often involves the shattering of dreams—the loss of the child they had dreamed of parenting. Sometimes there is the emotional or physical loss of the child as well. Yet of the families surveyed, only one experienced divorce and only two disrupted their adoptions permanently. All of these parents could site extreme, severe, and chronic stress for themselves as individuals and for the couple in their marriage relationship. Making it a priority to keep the marriage relationship healthy, strong, and continually growing brought benefits for some. Most, however, also shared that they developed strategies for taking good care of themselves as well as their hurt children. Two-thirds of the children in the sample were able to live in their adoptive home without recourse to temporary out-of-home care. Many parents talked of discovering strengths, establishing clearer priorities, and growing in new and unexpected ways.

None of the parents interviewed said they wished they had not adopted. The challenge of parenting for most was both exhausting and enlivening—like mountain climbing. What they wish for is a continuity of enlightened therapeutic support that they can access when they need it from a society that values them and supports them as the permanent healing families for its hurt children.

Glossary

Adoption Subsidy—financial assistance, medical coverage, and support services for families adopting special-needs children. It is best to have the child's eligibility confirmed and the general terms of the subsidy spelled out prior to placement, and requests for any adjustments made and confirmed before finalization.

Adoptive parent—a person who agrees to parent a child forever, as if the child had been born to him or her, and to whom full parental rights have been given by the court.

Attachment/bonding—In *a Child's Journey Through Placement*, Dr. Vera Fahlberg refers to *attachment* as the child's connection to the parent and *bonding* as the parent's connection with the child. Attached children trust a parent to take care of them, accept appropriate limits, and develop reciprocal behaviors. Bonded parents not only care for a child's needs and safety but also interact with them socially.

Attachment disorder—the impaired ability of a child to bond or to love. When adults in a child's life have been experienced as untrustworthy, children can have problems with attachment. They will not trust parental figures without testing them. The degree of testing will depend on where the child is on the attachment continuum: whether they have problems with attachment, are attachment disordered, or, in the extreme, are unattached. In *Hope for High Risk and Rage Filled Children: Reactive Attachment Disorder*, Dr. Foster Cline lists symptoms that almost all attachment-disordered children show:
- Self-abuse
- Cruelty to animals
- Cruelty to other children

- Inability to reciprocate affection, particularly with primary caregivers
- Inappropriate friendliness with strangers
- Speech problems
- Thought disorders, such as the inability to link cause and effect
- Problems with food (hoarding and gorging)
- Severe control battles at home and at school
- Crazy lying in the face of the obvious
- Few if any real friends

Attention Deficit Disorder (ADD), Attention Deficit Hyperactive Disorder (ADHD)—organically based conditions that result in a person finding it difficult to pay attention, be organized, and tolerate stress. People with ADD or ADHD act impulsively, suffer from mood swings, are distractible and hyperactive. Treatment of children with this condition usually involves medication, behavior modification, and encouragement to develop their high-energy talents.

Biological family, birth family, family of origin—all refer to the family into which the child was physically born.

Disrupt—ending the adoptive relationship emotionally and legally; either the parent or the child walks away from the other forever. Temporary placement of a child for residential treatment does not constitute an adoption disruption if contact is maintained. Confusion can arise because for a child to be eligible for some residential placements parents are required to relinquish guardianship to the Department of Social Services.

Dissociation—a defense mechanism whereby one detaches from the environment and focuses elsewhere in order to avoid being overwhelmed. When situations are so stressful that a person gets stuck in the process and therefore is functional on one level but not on another, dissociation can develop into a disorder.

Emotional abuse—when one person constantly denigrates another or uses the feelings of another to foster his or her own needs or feelings. Some examples are constantly telling a person he or she is stupid or incompetent, hurting a pet in front of the child who loves it, regularly making promises to do things for or with a child and not keeping those promises.

Fetal Alcohol Effect (FAE)—the effect the abuse of alcohol by a pregnant woman can have on her unborn child. Alcohol imbibed by the child through the placenta can cause dysfunction of the central nervous system and impair growth. The exact effect will depend on the stage of development of the fetus when the abuse occurs and the severity of the abuse.

Fetal Alcohol Syndrome (FAS)—the series of problems that can occur when a pregnant woman abuses alcohol. In addition to the results of Fetal Alcohol Effect, children with Fetal Alcohol Syndrome have distinct facial features and may have physical abnormalities, making FAS easier to diagnose than FAE. Michael Dorris's book *The Broken Cord* describes what it is like to parent a child with FAS.

Flashback—the involuntary replaying of a traumatic incident in the imagination. Although daydreaming is a natural occurrence for children, people who have been traumatized may see the trauma happening repeatedly in their daydreams and nightmares for a period of time after the event. They may experience flashbacks as an interruption to their thoughts or consciousness brought about by seeing someone, smelling something, or being somewhere that triggers a memory of the trauma. Not everyone with Post Traumatic Stress Syndrome has flashbacks, nor does everyone experience them the same way or with the same triggers.

Fost-adopt—placement in a foster home where the parents intend to adopt the child if/when parental rights are relinquished or terminated. It may also be referred to as an *at-risk placement* or sometimes *pre-adoptive placement*.

Foster parent—a person employed by a public agency, such as the Department of Social Services, or by a licensed private agency to parent a child during the period before the child can return to the birth home, is adopted, or moves into another placement. Sometimes foster-family placements are long-term, even lasting to adulthood.

Home study—the study an adoption agency does to discern the appropriateness of a family for adoption. It can involve the adoption worker meeting with the couple or single parent, and with the husband and wife separately. Those wanting to adopt may be asked to write a short autobiography. Group meetings with others preparing to adopt might be scheduled. Home study always includes a visit with the prospective parents and other members of the immediate family in the home, the submitting of references, and a doctor's assurance that the couple is healthy enough to take on such a long-term commitment. At the end of the process the worker must have a sense of the strengths, weaknesses, and expectations of the couple, and the kind of child appropriate for them. In the case of older child adoption, the worker will be concerned about whether their support system, ability to endure conflict, and resilience make them good prospective parents. After the home study the worker will recommend that the couple be allowed to adopt or not.

Learning disability—refers not to intelligence but to the way a person absorbs and retains information. Most learning stimuli in the classroom are auditory and visual. Children with learning disabilities do not always learn as well from auditory or visual stimuli, or cannot manage a multiplicity of stimuli. Since auditory and visual communicating is used almost to the exclusion of the tactile (touch) in education, and people are expected to be able to focus and screen out extraneous stimuli, not being able to do so is a disability. Learning disabilities can be functional and/or organic. Functional disabilities can be caused by such things as unresolved grief, situation anxiety, and the tremendous effort it takes to forget past hurts.

Least restrictive environment—the environment that provides children with enough structure so that they will be prevented from hurting themselves or others and be able to receive the treatment and education they need to develop their potential. In this sense, a hospital is the most restrictive environment and a family is the least restrictive environment for a child. In relation to educational needs, the least restrictive environment refers to the environment that provides enough structure for the child to be able to learn. Some children can learn in a regular classroom; others need a smaller student-teacher ratio or a more controlled environment. The least restrictive environment means just enough structure and no more. Reviews of placement are regularly scheduled, and as children need less structure they are moved to a less structured environment.

Pre-adoptive placement—the time after a child has been placed with an adoptive family and before the adoption has been finalized.

Post Traumatic Stress Syndrome—reaction to a trauma, such as witnessing a murder, suddenly losing one's parents, or being sodomized or raped, which strips a child of a sense of invincibility and safety. The child is left feeling vulnerable and anxious. When the person least expects it, he or she can reexperience the trauma in a flashback. The predictability of life can no longer be trusted.

Psychological parent—anyone who has cared for the child as a parent does and with whom the child has bonded as if to a parent.

Psycho-social dwarfism—failure to grow because the child lives in fear and deprivation. This condition may reverse itself when the child is moved to a safe and nurturing environment.

Relinquishment of parental rights—when a parent willingly and legally, usually with a court appearance, gives up his or her right to parent the child. In some states it is called *voluntary termination of parental rights.*

Residential school—a placement that can be made by the Department of Social or Mental-Health Services but usually is made through the school system. The child lives, goes to school, and receives therapy on the same grounds. As the child progresses, he or she might attend regular school and work in the community but remains at the same residence until the placement is terminated.

Residential treatment center—an out-of-home therapeutic placement generally referred through the Department of Mental Health. The child lives, receives therapy, and usually goes to school in an intensely therapeutic milieu that is not as restrictive as a hospital but is more restrictive than a residential school.

Sexual abuse—emotional or physical coercion for sexual interaction and gratification. It may include physical contact or not. The sexual abuse of children involves such coerced interaction by an adult or another child in a position of trust or power.

Splitting—separating of two things that ought to go together. Children go through a period of splitting when they perceive their parent as, for example, a good mom or a bad mom depending on whether she is taking them to the circus or requiring that they do their chores. Eventually most children realize that both these aspects—"good" and "bad"—are in the same person, and they grow out of their split thinking. For adopted children this is more difficult because there are, in fact, at least two moms. Often they are stuck in split thinking that the mom they are with is the bad mom because she disciplines them, and they fantasize their birth mom as the good mom who would let them do whatever they want.

Exterior splitting results when people responsible for a child do not respect and communicate with each other so the child is able to set them against each other. For example, the child convinces the teacher that his parents are the problem. Or, by behaving like an angel when Dad gets home and a devil the rest of the day, a child convinces Dad that Mom is the problem. The child thus causes a split in his or her environment and escapes through the crack; that is, by being perceived as the victim, the child is not held responsible for his or her behavior.

Termination of parental rights—involuntary or voluntary ending of the parent-child relationship. Involuntary termination occurs when, after a significant period of time, the court determines that a parent has failed to show the capability and serious intent to make the changes necessary to be able to parent his or her child safely. Voluntary termination occurs when birth or adoptive parents make the decision that they can no longer parent the child.

The custody of the child can then be transferred by the court to a public or private agency or, rarely, to another individual.

Therapeutic foster family—a foster family that parents very disturbed children and receives intensive training and therapeutic support services in order to provide the child with what he or she needs.

Therapist—a mental-health professional, usually with a graduate degree in social work, psychology, or counseling. Only psychiatrists can prescribe medication. Not all therapists are aware of the complicated dynamics and challenges presented by older adopted children and their families. References from other adoptive families, schools, and therapists can be helpful.

Selected Bibliography

Alexander-Roberts, Colleen. *The ADHD Parenting Handbook: Practical Advice for Parents and Professionals.* Dallas, Tex.: Taylor Publishing Co., 1994.

Babb, L. Anne, and Rita Laws. *Adopting and Advocating for the Special Needs Child.* Westport, Conn.: Greenwood Publishing Group, 1997.

Barth, R. P., and M. Berry. *Adoption and Disruption: Rates, Risks, and Responses.* Hawthorne, N.Y.: Aldine D. Gruyter, 1988.

Brodzinsky, D. M., M. D. Schechter, and R. Marantz. *Being Adopted: The Lifelong Search for Self.* New York: Doubleday, 1992.

Carney, A. *No More Here and There: Adopting the Older Child.* Chapel Hill, N.C.: The University of North Carolina Press, 1976.

Cline, F. W. *Hope for High Risk and Rage Filled Children.* Evergreen, Colo.: EC Publications, 1992.

Delaney, R. J. *Fostering Changes: Treating Attachment Disordered Foster Children.* Fort. Collins, Colo.: Walter J. Corbett, 1991.

————, and F. Kunstal. *Troubled Transplants: Unconventional Strategies for Helping Disturbed Foster and Adopted Children.* Portland, Maine: University of Southern Maine, 1993.

Fahlberg, V. *A Child's Journey Through Placement.* Indianapolis, Ind.: Perspectives Press, 1991.

Fitzgerald, H. *The Grieving Child: A Parent's Guide.* New York: Simon and Schuster, 1992.

Gitlin, H. J. *Adoptions: An Attorney's Guide to Helping Adoptive Parents,* Woodstock, Ill.: Callaghan and Co. 1987.

Grabe, P. V., ed. *Adoption Resources for Mental Health Professionals.* New Brunswick, N.J.: Transaction Publishers, 1990.

Jewett, Claudia L. *Adopting the Older Child.* Boston, Mass.: Harvard Common Press, 1978.

————. *Helping Children Cope with Separation and Loss.* Harvard, Mass.: Harvard Common Press, 1982.

Keck, G. C., and R. M. Kupecky. *Adopting the Hurt Child: Hope for Families with Special Needs Kids, A Guide for Parents and Professionals,* Colorado Springs, Colo.: Pinon Press, 1995.

Kulp, J. *Families at Risk: A Guide to Understanding and Protecting Children and Care Providers Involved in Out-of-Home or Adoptive Care.* Minneapolis, Minn.: Better Endings, New Beginnings, 1993.

Lifton, B. J. *Journey of the Adopted Self: A Quest for Wholeness.* New York: Harper & Row, 1994.

McCreight, Brenda. *Recognizing and Managing Children with Fetal Alcohol Syndrome/Fetal Alcohol Effects: A Guidebook.* Washington, D.C.: Child Welfare League Press, 1997.

McKelvey, C. A., and Dr. J. E. Stevens. *Adoption Crisis: The Truth Behind Adoption and Foster Care.* Golden, Colo.: Fulcrum Publishing, 1994.

McNamara, J. *Sexually Reactive Children in Adoption and Foster Care.* Greensboro, N.C.: Family Resources, 1992.

————, ed. *Bruised Before Birth: Parenting Children Exposed to Substance Abuse.* London: British Association for Fostering and Adoption, 1995.

————, and B. McNamara, eds. *Adoption and the Sexually Abused Child.* Portland, Maine: University of Southern Maine, 1990.

O'Hanlon, T. *Adoption Subsidy: A Guide for Adoptive Parents.* Columbus, Ohio: New Roots, 1995.

Paterson, Katherine. *The Great Gilly Hopkins.* New York: Harper Collins, 1987.

Peterson, Janelle. *The Invisible Road: Parental Insights to Attachment Disorders.* 1994.

Pohl, C., and K. Harris. *Transracial Adoption: Children and Parents Speak.* New York: Franklin Watts, 1992.

Stein, L. M., and J. L. Hoopes. *Identity Formation in the Adopted Adolescent: The Delaware Family Study.* New York: Child Welfare League of America, 1985.

Terr, Lenore, M.D. *Too Scared to Cry: Psychic Trauma in Childhood.* New York: Harper & Row, 1990.

Van Gulden, H., and L. Bartels-Rabb. *Real Parents, Real Children: Parenting the Adopted Child.* New York: Crossroads, 1993.

Verrier, N. N. *The Primal Wound: Understanding the Adopted Child.* Baltimore, Md.: Gateway Press, 1993.

Welch, M. G. *Holding Time.* New York: Simon and Schuster, 1988.

National Resources

Adoptive Families of America
2309 Como Ave.
St. Paul, MN 55108
800-372-330

CAP Book (Children Awaiting
   Parents)
700 Exchange St.
Rochester, NY 14608
716-232-5110

National Adoption Center (NAC)
1500 Walnut St., Suite 701
Philadelphia, PA 19102
215-735-9988

National Adoption Information
   Clearninghouse
5640 Nicholson Lane, Suite 300
Rockville, MD 20852
301-231-6512

National Council for Single
   Adoptive Parents
P.O. Box 15084
Chevy Chase, MD 20825
202-966-6367

North American Council on
   Adoptable Children (NACAC)
1821 University Ave., Suite N-498
St. Paul, MN 55104
612-644-3036

Parent Network for the Post-Insti-
   tutionalized Child
Box 613
Meadow Lands, PA 15347
412-222-1766

Spaulding for Children/National
   Resource for Special Needs
   Adoption (NRCSNA)
16250 Northland Drive, Suite 120
Southville, MI 48075
248-443-7080